# Four Corners

## Jack C. Richards · David Bohlke

**1**

## Student's Book

CAMBRIDGE UNIVERSITY PRESS
Cambridge, New York, Melbourne, Madrid, Cape Town,
Singapore, São Paulo, Delhi, Mexico City

Cambridge University Press
32 Avenue of the Americas, New York, NY 10013-2473, USA

www.cambridge.org
Information on this title: www.cambridge.org/9780521126151

First published 2012
3rd printing 2013

Printed in Hong Kong, China, by Golden Cup Printing Company Limited

*A catalog record for this publication is available from the British Library.*

ISBN  978-0-521-12615-1  Student's Book 1 with Self-study CD-ROM
ISBN  978-0-521-12654-0  Workbook 1
ISBN  978-0-521-12646-5  Teacher's Edition 1 with Assessment CD-ROM
ISBN  978-0-521-12640-3  Class Audio CDs 1
ISBN  978-0-521-12619-9  Classware 1
ISBN  978-0-521-12638-0  DVD 1

For a full list of components, visit www.cambridge.org/fourcorners

Art direction, book design, photo research, and layout services: Adventure House, NYC
Audio production: CityVox, NYC
Video production: Steadman Productions

# Authors' acknowledgments

Many people contributed to the development of *Four Corners*. The authors and publisher would like to particularly thank the following **reviewers**:

Nele Noe, **Academy for Educational Development, Qatar Independent Secondary School for Girls**, Doha, Qatar; Yuan-hsun Chuang, **Soo Chow University**, Taipei, Taiwan; Celso Frade and Sonia Maria Baccari de Godoy, **Associaçao Alumni**, São Paulo, Brazil; Pablo Stucchi, **Antonio Raimondi School** and **Instituto San Ignacio de Loyola**, Lima, Peru; Kari Miller, **Binational Center**, Quito, Ecuador; Alex K. Oliveira, **Boston University**, Boston, MA, USA; Elisabeth Blom, **Casa Thomas Jefferson**, Brasilia, Brazil; Henry Grant, **CCBEU – Campinas**, Campinas, Brazil; Maria do Rosário, **CCBEU – Franca**, Franca, Brazil; Ane Cibele Palma, **CCBEU Inter Americano**, Curitiba, Brazil; Elen Flavia Penques da Costa, **Centro de Cultura Idiomas – Taubate**, Taubate, Brazil; Inara Lúcia Castillo Couto, **CEL LEP – São Paulo**, São Paulo, Brazil; Geysa de Azevedo Moreira, **Centro Cultural Brasil Estados Unidos (CCBEU Belém)**, Belém, Brazil; Sonia Patricia Cardoso, **Centro de Idiomas Universidad Manuela Beltrán**, Barrio Cedritos, Colombia; Geraldine Itiago Losada, **Centro Universitario Grupo Sol (Musali)**, Mexico City, Mexico; Nick Hilmers, **DePaul University**, Chicago, IL, USA; Monica L. Montemayor Menchaca, **EDIMSA**, Metepec, Mexico; Angela Whitby, **Edu-Idiomas Language School**, Cholula, Puebla, Mexico; Mary Segovia, **El Monte Rosemead Adult School**, Rosemead, CA, USA; Dr. Deborah Aldred, **ELS Language Centers, Middle East Region**, Abu Dhabi, United Arab Emirates; Leslie Lott, **Embassy CES**, Ft. Lauderdale, FL, USA; M. Martha Lengeling, **Escuela de Idiomas**, Guanajuato, Mexico; Pablo Frias, **Escuela de Idiomas UNAPEC**, Santo Domingo, Dominican Republic; Tracy Vanderhoek, **ESL Language Center**, Toronto, Canada; Kris Vicca and Michael McCollister, **Feng Chia University**, Taichung, Taiwan; Flávia Patricia do Nascimento Martins, **First Idiomas**, Sorocaba, Brazil; Andrea Taylor, **Florida State University in Panama**, Panamá, Panama; Carlos Lizárraga González, **Groupo Educativo Angloamericano**, Mexico City, Mexico; Dr. Martin Endley, **Hanyang University**, Seoul, Korea; Mauro Luiz Pinheiro, **IBEU Ceará**, Ceará, Brazil; Ana Lúcia da Costa Maia de Almeida, **IBEU Copacabana**, Copacabana, Brazil; Ana Lucia Almeida, Elisa Borges, **IBEU Rio**, Rio de Janeiro, Brazil; Maristela Silva, **ICBEU Manaus**, Manaus, Brazil; Magaly Mendes Lemos, **ICBEU São José dos Campos**, São José dos Campos, Brazil; Augusto Pelligrini Filho, **ICBEU São Luis**, São Luis, Brazil; Leonardo Mercado, **ICPNA**, Lima, Peru; Lucia Rangel Lugo, **Instituto Tecnológico de San Luis Potosí**, San Luis Potosí, Mexico; Maria Guadalupe Hernández Lozada, **Instituto Tecnológico de Tlalnepantla**, Tlalnepantla de Baz, Mexico; Greg Jankunis, **International Education Service**, Tokyo, Japan; Karen Stewart, **International House Veracruz**, Veracruz, Mexico; George Truscott, **Kinki University**, Osaka, Japan; Bo-Kyung Lee, **Hankuk University of Foreign Studies**, Seoul, Korea; Andy Burki, **Korea University, International Foreign Language School**, Seoul, Korea; Jinseo Noh, **Kwangwoon University**, Seoul, Korea; Nadezhda Nazarenko, **Lone Star College**, Houston, TX, USA; Carolyn Ho, **Lone Star College-Cy-Fair**, Cypress, TX, USA; Alice Ya-fen Chou, **National Taiwan University of Science and Technology**, Taipei, Taiwan; Gregory Hadley, **Niigata University of International and Information Studies, Department of Information Culture**, Niigata-shi, Japan; Raymond Dreyer, **Northern Essex Community College**, Lawrence, MA, USA; Mary Keter Terzian Megale, **One Way Línguas-Suzano**, São Paulo, Brazil; Jason Moser, **Osaka Shoin Joshi University**, Kashiba-shi, Japan; Bonnie Cheeseman, **Pasadena Community College** and **UCLA American Language Center**, Los Angeles, CA, USA; Simon Banha, **Phil Young's English School**, Curitiba, Brazil; Oh Jun Il, **Pukyong National University**, Busan, Korea; Carmen Gehrke, **Quatrum English Schools**, Porto Alegre, Brazil; Atsuko K. Yamazaki, **Shibaura Institute of Technology**, Saitama, Japan; Wen hsiang Su, **Shi Chien University, Kaohsiung Campus**, Kaohsiung, Taiwan; Richmond Stroupe, **Soka University, World Language Center**, Hachioji, Tokyo, Japan; Lynne Kim, **Sun Moon University (Institute for Language Education)**, Cheon An City, Chung Nam, Korea; Hiroko Nishikage, **Taisho University**, Tokyo, Japan; Diana Peña Munoz and Zaira Kuri, **The Anglo**, Mexico City, Mexico; Alistair Campbell, **Tokyo University of Technology**, Tokyo, Japan; Song-won Kim, **TTI (Teacher's Training Institute)**, Seoul, Korea; Nancy Alarcón, **UNAM FES Zaragoza Language Center**, Mexico City, Mexico; Laura Emilia Fierro López, **Universidad Autónoma de Baja California**, Mexicali, Mexico; María del Rocío Domíngeuz Gaona, **Universidad Autónoma de Baja California**, Tijuana, Mexico; Saul Santos Garcia, **Universidad Autónoma de Nayarit**, Nayarit, Mexico; Christian Meléndez, **Universidad Católica de El Salvador**, San Salvador, El Salvador; Irasema Mora Pablo, **Universidad de Guanajuato**, Guanajuato, Mexico; Alberto Peto, **Universidad de Oxaca**, Tehuantepec, Mexico; Carolina Rodriguez Beltan, **Universidad Manuela Beltrán, Centro Colombo Americano**, and **Universidad Jorge Tadeo Lozano**, Bogotá, Colombia; Nidia Milena Molina Rodriguez, **Universidad Manuela Beltrán** and **Universidad Militar Nueva Granada**, Bogotá, Colombia; Yolima Perez Arias, **Universidad Nacional de Colombia**, Bogota, Colombia; Héctor Vázquez García, **Universidad Nacional Autónoma de Mexico**, Mexico City, Mexico; Pilar Barrera, **Universidad Técnica de Ambato**, Ambato, Ecuador; Deborah Hulston, **University of Regina**, Regina, Canada; Rebecca J. Shelton, **Valparaiso University, Interlink Language Center**, Valparaiso, IN, USA; Tae Lee, **Yonsei University**, Seodaemun-gu, Seoul, Korea; Claudia Thereza Nascimento Mendes, **York Language Institute**, Rio de Janeiro, Brazil; Jamila Jenny Hakam, **ELT Consultant**, Muscat, Oman; Stephanie Smith, **ELT Consultant**, Austin, TX, USA.

The authors would also like to thank the Four Corners editorial, production, and new media teams, as well as the Cambridge University Press staff and advisors around the world for their contributions and tireless commitment to quality.

# Scope and sequence

| LEVEL 1 | Learning outcomes | Grammar | Vocabulary |
|---|---|---|---|
| **Welcome Unit** Pages 2–3 <br> **Classroom language** Page 4 | **Students can . . .** <br> ☑ introduce themselves and others <br> ☑ say hello and good-bye | | |

| Functional language | Listening and Pronunciation | Reading and Writing | Speaking |
|---|---|---|---|
| **Interactions:** <br> Saying hello <br> Saying good-bye | | | • Introductions <br> • Greetings |
| **Interactions:** <br> Asking for spelling | **Listening:** <br> Spelling names <br> **Pronunciation:** <br> Contractions | **Reading:** <br> "Famous Names" <br> An article <br> **Writing:** <br> My name | • Class introductions and greetings <br> • *Keep talking:* Name circle <br> • Class name list <br> • Guessing game about famous people <br> • *Keep talking:* "Find the differences" activity about jobs and cities <br> • Quiz about celebrities |
| **Interactions:** <br> Asking for someone's <br> phone number <br> Asking for someone's <br> email address | **Listening:** <br> Directory Assistance <br> calls <br> Information forms <br> People I know <br> **Pronunciation:** <br> Word stress | **Reading:** <br> "People in My Life" <br> Photo captions <br> **Writing:** <br> My friends | • True and false information about people <br> • *Keep talking:* Interviews with new identities <br> • Class survey for new contact information <br> • Information exchange about family members <br> • *Keep talking:* Family trees <br> • Presentation about friends |
| **Interactions:** <br> Asking what <br> something is | **Listening:** <br> Things around the <br> classroom <br> Favorite things <br> **Pronunciation:** <br> Plurals | **Reading:** <br> "What's your favorite <br> item of clothing?" <br> A webpage <br> **Writing:** <br> My favorite thing | • Questions and answers about personal items <br> • *Keep talking:* Things in the closet <br> • Memory game about everyday items <br> • Personal items and their owners <br> • *Keep talking:* "Find the differences" activity about clothing colors <br> • Presentation of favorite things |
| **Interactions:** <br> Asking the time | **Listening:** <br> Times of different <br> events <br> Angela's routine <br> **Pronunciation:** <br> Reduction of *to* | **Reading:** <br> "What's your favorite <br> day of the week?" <br> A message board <br> **Writing:** <br> About my weekend | • Survey about getting to school and work <br> • *Keep talking:* Transportation facts <br> • Interview about the times of specific events <br> • Interview about routines <br> • *Keep talking:* "Find someone who" activity about routines <br> • Survey about busy weekends |
| **Interactions:** <br> Declining help <br> Accepting help | **Listening:** <br> Shopping <br> Favorite websites <br> **Pronunciation:** <br> Stress in numbers | **Reading:** <br> "Fun Online Activities" <br> An article <br> **Writing:** <br> Let's chat | • Comparison of online habits <br> • *Keep talking:* Interview about online habits <br> • Role play of a shopping situation <br> • Interview about leisure activities <br> • *Keep talking:* Interviews about fun activities <br> • Discussion about favorite websites |
| **Interactions:** <br> Asking for someone on <br> the phone <br> Having someone wait | **Listening:** <br> Telephone calls <br> Ads for overseas <br> programs <br> **Pronunciation:** <br> *Can* and *can't* | **Reading:** <br> "Overseas <br> Opportunities" <br> A magazine article <br> **Writing:** <br> My abilities | • "Find someone who" activity about jobs <br> • *Keep talking:* Memory game about jobs <br> • Role play of a phone call <br> • Interview about abilities <br> • *Keep talking:* Board game about abilities <br> • Discussion about study and work programs |

| LEVEL 1 | Learning outcomes | Grammar | Vocabulary |
|---|---|---|---|

| Functional language | Listening and Pronunciation | Reading and Writing | Speaking |
|---|---|---|---|
| **Interactions:** Expressing dislikes Expressing likes | **Listening:** Food preferences A typical Swedish meal **Pronunciation:** Word stress | **Reading:** "My Favorite Food" An article **Writing:** A typical meal | • Survey about meals • *Keep talking:* Recipes • Information exchange about food preferences • Comparison of eating habits • *Keep talking:* Discussion about eating habits • Interview about favorite food |
| **Interactions:** Asking for directions | **Listening:** GPS directions Tourist information **Pronunciation:** Word stress | **Reading:** "Monterey Bay Aquarium" A poster **Writing:** Group poster | • Information exchange with maps • *Keep talking:* Information gap activity with neighborhood maps • Role play about directions • Interview about places in town • *Keep talking:* Description of an unusual zoo • Presentation about a city attraction |
| **Interactions:** Asking if someone can talk now Explaining that you can't talk now | **Listening:** Sound effects Telephone calls **Pronunciation:** Intonation in questions | **Reading:** "Status Updates" A micro-blog **Writing:** My status update | • Guessing game about people's actions • *Keep talking:* Interpretations of actions • Role play of a phone call • "Find someone who" activity about things people are doing these days • *Keep talking:* Guessing game about who's doing what • Speculations about someone's activities |
| **Interactions:** Showing that you're listening Expressing surprise | **Listening:** Diana's week Matt's busy week **Pronunciation:** Simple past -ed endings | **Reading:** "Matt's Movie Reviews" Blog posts **Writing:** A blog post | • Information exchange about last weekend • *Keep talking:* Picture story • Role play of surprising conversations • Interview about routine events in the past • *Keep talking:* Memories • "Find someone who" activity about past activities |
| **Interactions:** Reacting to good news Reacting to bad news | **Listening:** A short trip Three vacations **Pronunciation:** Reduction of *did you* | **Reading:** "Travel Tales" Blog posts **Writing:** A postcard | • Interview about where you were • *Keep talking:* Interview about school trips • Class exchange of personal news • Information exchange about vacations • *Keep talking:* Speculations about a vacation • Presentation of postcards |
| **Interactions:** Declining an invitation Accepting an invitation | **Listening:** Invitations A "Sweet 16" birthday party **Pronunciation:** Reduction of *going to* | **Reading:** "Birthday Traditions" An article **Writing:** A thank-you note | • Information exchange about special days • *Keep talking:* Weekend plans • Class invitations • Discussion of plans for three scenarios • *Keep talking:* Plan for a party • Discussion about birthday traditions |

# Welcome

## 1 Introducing yourself

**A** 🔊 Listen and practice.

**Simon:** Hello. I'm Simon.
**Chen:** Hi, Simon. My name is Chen.
Nice to meet you.
**Simon:** Nice to meet you, too.

**B Pair work** Introduce yourselves.

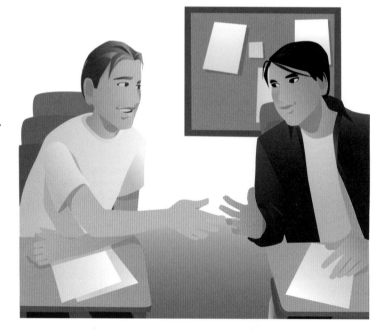

## 2 Introducing someone else

**A** 🔊 Listen and practice.

**Simon:** Chen, this is my friend Sofia.
**Sofia:** Hi, Chen. Nice to meet you.
**Chen:** Nice to meet you, too, Sofia.

**B Group work** Introduce your partner from Exercise 1 to another classmate.

# 3 Hi and bye

**A** 🔊 Listen and practice.

**Simon:** Hi, Chen!
**Chen:** Good morning, Simon! How are you?
**Simon:** I'm fine, thanks. And you?
**Chen:** Fine, thank you.

**Simon:** See you later, Chen!
**Chen:** Bye, Simon!

**B** 🔊 Listen to the expressions. Then practice the conversation again with the new expressions.

| *Saying hello* |
| --- |
| Hi. |
| Hello. |
| Good morning.  |
| Good afternoon.  |
| Good evening.  |

| *Saying good-bye* |
| --- |
| Bye. |
| Good-bye. |
| See you. |
| See you later. |
| See you tomorrow. |

**C** **Class activity** Say hello to your classmates and ask how they are. Then say good-bye.

| I can *introduce myself and others.* ☑ |
| --- |
| I can *say hello and good-bye.* ☑ |

3

# Classroom language

Pair work

Group work

Class activity

Compare answers.

Cover the picture.

Go to page 12.

Ask and answer questions.

Interview your partner.

Role-play the situation.

# New friends

## Warm-up

### Popular names in the United States

1. Jacob
2. Michael
3. Ethan
4. Joshua
5. Daniel

1. Emma
2. Isabella
3. Emily
4. Madison
5. Ava

*Source:* www.ssa.gov/OACT/babynames/

**A** Check (✓) the popular names.

**B** Say ten popular names in your country.

## 1 Language in context First day of class

🔊 Listen to Ms. Peters meet her students on the first day of class. Underline the names.

> Hello, everyone. I'm your teacher, Ms. Peters. My first name is Linda.

> Hi. What's your name?

> My name is Maria Gomez.

> Hi. I'm Maria. What are your names?

> What are their names?

> My name is Ricardo.

> And I'm Yoko. Nice to meet you.

> Her name is Yoko. His name is Ricardo.

## 2 Vocabulary Names and titles

**A** 🔊 Listen and repeat.

first name   middle name   last / family name

**Jennifer Ann Wilson**

full name

Miss Gomez = a single woman

Mrs. Chow = a married woman

Ms. Peters = a single or married woman

Mr. Adams = a single or married man

**B Pair work** Complete the sentences with your own information. Then compare answers.

My first name is _____ .  My full name is _____ .

My family name is _____ .  My teacher's name is _____ .

# 3 Grammar 🔊 The verb *be*; possessive adjectives

| What is (What's) | your name? his name? her name? | **My** name **is** Maria. **His** name **is** Ricardo. **Her** name **is** Yoko. |
|---|---|---|
| **What are** | your names? their names? | **Our** names **are** Maria and Jason. **Their** names **are** Ricardo and Yoko. |

**A** Circle the correct words. Then compare with a partner.

1. Maria is a student. **His** / **(Her)** last name is Gomez.
2. Ms. Peters **is** / **are** our teacher. **Her** / **Their** first name is Linda.
3. My name is Jason. What's **our** / **your** name?
4. Anna and Bruce **is** / **are** students. **Her** / **Their** teacher is Miss Brown.
5. Their first names **is** / **are** Yoko and Ricardo.
6. Hello, everyone. I'm Miss Diaz. What are **your** / **his** names?

**B** Complete the conversation with the correct words. Then practice in a group.

A: Hello. Welcome to English class. What _____*is*_____ your name, please?

B: _____ name is Pam.

A: And what's _____ last name, Pam?

B: My last name _____ Nelson.

A: OK. And _____ is *your* name?

C: Ji-ah. _____ family name is Lee.

# 4 Speaking My name is . . .

**A Class activity** Meet your classmates. Say your first and last name.

A: *Hello. My name is Oscar Martinez. What's your name?*
B: *Hi. My name is Susana Harris.*
A: *It's nice to meet you.*
B: *Nice to meet you, too.*

**B** Share your information.

A: *What's his name?*
B: *His name is Oscar Martinez. What's her name?*
A: *Sorry, I don't know.*

# 5 Keep talking!

Go to page 125 for more practice.

*I can ask for and say names.* ✓

# B How do you spell it?

## 1 The alphabet

**A** 🔊 Listen and repeat.

| A | B | C | D | E | F | G | H | I | J | K | L | M |

| N | O | P | Q | R | S | T | U | V | W | X | Y | Z |

**B Pair work** Say a letter. Your partner points to it. Take turns.

## 2 Interactions    Spelling names

**A** 🔊 Listen and practice.

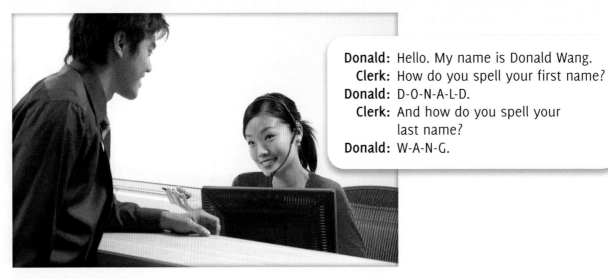

**Donald:** Hello. My name is Donald Wang.
**Clerk:** How do you spell your first name?
**Donald:** D-O-N-A-L-D.
**Clerk:** And how do you spell your last name?
**Donald:** W-A-N-G.

### Asking for spelling

How do you spell your first name?
How do you spell your last name?

**B Pair work** Practice the conversation again with these names.

John Evans    Cindy Douglas    Antonia Lopez    Richard Wu

**A:** *Hello. My name is John Evans.*
**B:** *Hello, John. How do you spell your first name?*
**A:** *J-O-H-N.*
**B:** *And how do you spell . . . ?*

# 3 Listening Spell it!

**A** 🔊 Listen to four people spell their names. Check (✓) the correct answers.

1. ☑ Steven    2. ☐ Dina    3. ☐ Kelly    4. ☐ Bryan
   ☐ Stephen      ☐ Dena      ☐ Kerry      ☐ Brian

**B** 🔊 Listen to the conversations. Write the names.

1.

2.

3.

4.

5.

6.

# 4 Speaking A class list

**Class activity** Ask your classmates for their names. Make a list.

A: *What's your first name?*
B: *Tyler.*
A: *How do you spell it?*
B: *T-Y-L-E-R.*
A: *And what's your last name?*
B: *Larsen.*

| First names | Last names |
| --- | --- |
| Tyler | Larsen |
| Lindsey | Fisher |
| Marcela | Perez |
| Evan | Howley |
| Dmitri | Benos |

*I can spell names.* ☑

# C Are you a student?

## 1 Vocabulary Interesting jobs

**A** 🔊 Listen and repeat.

Gael García Bernal is an **actor**.
He's from Mexico.

Jeon Do-yeon is an **actress**.
She's from South Korea.

Alex Hornest is an **artist**.
He's from Brazil.

Brooklyn Decker is a **model**.
She's from the United States.

Lang Lang is a **musician**.
He's from China.

Diana Krall is a **singer**.
She's from Canada.

**B Pair work** Name other people for each job.

A: *Jet Li is an actor.*
B: *Yes. And Cate Blanchett is an actress.*

## 2 Conversation My friend the musician

🔊 Listen and practice.

**Sandy:** Hey, Jacob!
**Jacob:** Oh, hi, Sandy. How's it going?
**Sandy:** Good, thanks. This is my friend Kevin.
**Jacob:** Hi. Nice to meet you.
**Kevin:** Nice to meet you, Jacob.
**Jacob:** Are you a student here?
**Kevin:** No, I'm not. I'm a musician.
**Sandy:** Kevin is from England.
**Jacob:** Oh? Are you from London?
**Kevin:** No, I'm not. I'm from Liverpool.

# 3 Grammar  Subject pronouns; *yes / no* questions with *be*

| | |
|---|---|
| I'm a musician. | **Am I** in your class? |
| | Yes, **you are**.     No, **you're not**. / No, **you aren't**. |
| You're a student. | **Are you** from London? |
| | Yes, **I am**.     No, **I'm not**. |
| Kevin **is** from Liverpool. | **Is he** a singer? |
| He's from Liverpool. | Yes, **he is**.     No, **he's not**. / No, **he isn't**. |
| Sandy **is** a student. | **Is she** from Canada? |
| She's a student. | Yes, **she is**.     No, **she's not**. / No, **she isn't**. |
| Liverpool **is** in England. | **Is your** name John? |
| It's in England. | Yes, **it is**.     No, **it's not**. / No, **it isn't**. |

*Contractions*   I'm = I am     you're = you are     he's = he is     she's = she is     it's = it is

**A** Match the questions and the answers. Then practice with a partner.

1. Is your first name Jacob? __*d*__
2. Are you from Liverpool? _____
3. Is she from the United States? _____
4. Is she a musician? _____
5. Is Will Smith an actor? _____
6. Is Caracas in Peru? _____

a. No, I'm not. I'm from London.
b. Yes, he is. He's a singer, too.
c. No, she's not. She's an artist.
d. Yes, it is. And my last name is King.
e. No, it's not. It's in Venezuela.
f. Yes, she is. She's from California.

**B** Complete the conversations with the correct words. Then practice with a partner.

1. **A:** _____*Is*_____ your first name Don?
   **B:** No, _____ not. It's Jeff.

2. **A:** _____ you from Mexico?
   **B:** Yes, I _____ . I'm from Mexico City.

3. **A:** _____ your teacher from England?
   **B:** No, she _____ .

4. **A:** _____ you a model?
   **B:** No, _____ not. I'm a singer.

# 4 Pronunciation  Contractions

Listen and repeat. Notice the reduction of contractions.

I am → I'm        he is → he's        it is → it's        are not → aren't

you are → you're        she is → she's        is not → isn't

# 5 Speaking  Ten questions

**Group work** Think of a famous person with a job from Exercise 1. Your group asks ten questions and guesses the name. Take turns.

**A:** *Is the person a man?*
**B:** *No, she's not.*
**C:** *Is she an actress?*

# 6 Keep talking!

Student A go to page 126 and Student B go to page 128 for more practice.

*I can* talk about where people are from and what they do.

## 1 Reading

**A** Look at the pictures. What are their names?

**B** Read the article. Are they all singers?

# ★ Famous Names

Actor **Tom Cruise** uses his middle name as his last name. His full name is Thomas Cruise Mapother. Tom is short for Thomas.

**Zhang Ziyi** is an actress from China. Zhang isn't her first name. It's her family name. In China, family names come first.

**Shakira** is a singer from Colombia. She uses only her first name. Her full name is Shakira Isabel Mebarak Ripoll.

**Jay-Z** is a hip-hop singer from the United States. Jay-Z is his nickname. His real name is Shawn Corey Carter.

**Kaká** is a soccer player from Brazil. His full name is Ricardo Izecson dos Santos Leite. Kaká is his nickname.

**Madonna** is not a nickname for this singer. It's her first name. Her full name is Madonna Louise Veronica Ciccone.

**C** Read the article again. Complete the sentences with the correct words.

1. Tom Cruise uses his ____*middle*____ name as his last name.
2. Shakira uses only her _____ name.
3. Ricardo Izecson dos Santos Leite's _____ is Kaká.
4. Ziyi is not Zhang Ziyi's _____ name.
5. Jay-Z's _____ name is Shawn Corey Carter.
6. Madonna Louise Veronica Ciccone is Madonna's _____ name.

**D** **Pair work** Tell your partner about another famous person's name.

*"Rain is a singer, actor, and model from South Korea. Rain is his nickname. His real name is Jeong Ji-hoon."*

# 2 **Writing** My name

**A** Write sentences about your name. Use the model to help you.

> ### My Name
> My full name is Anthony Steven Johnson. My nickname is Big Tony. Tony is short for Anthony. My middle name is Steven, and my last name is Johnson.

**B Group work** Tell your group about your name.

# 3 **Speaking** Celebrity quiz

**A Pair work** Ask and answer the questions about celebrities.

1. He's an actor from Hong Kong. His initials are J. C. What's his name?

   *"His name is Jackie Chan."*

2. She's an actress from Spain. Her last name is Cruz. What's her first name?

3. He's a soccer player from England. His first name is David. What's his last name?

4. She's an actress and singer. Her nickname is J-Lo. What's her name?

5. He's an actor from Australia. His first name is Russell. What's his last name?

6. She's an actress from the United States. Her last name is Jolie? What's her first name?

**B Pair work** Create a quiz. Write three sentences about a celebrity.

> He's a tennis player.
> He's from Switzerland.
> His first name is Roger.

**C Group work** Say your sentences to another pair. They guess the celebrity. Take turns.

    A: *He's a tennis player.*
    B: *Is he Rafael Nadal?*
    A: *No, he isn't. He's from Switzerland.*

> *I can discuss people's names and jobs.* ☑

# Wrap-up

## 1 Quick pair review

**Lesson A  Do you remember?** What are your classmates' last names? Answer with the information you remember. You have two minutes.

A: *Her last name is Fernandes.*
B: *Yes, it is. And his first name is Oscar. What's his last name?*
A: *It's Medina.*

**Lesson B  Test your partner!** Say your full name. Can your partner write it correctly? Check his or her answer. You have two minutes.

| First name | Middle name | Last / Family name |
| --- | --- | --- |
| | | |

**Lesson C  Brainstorm!** Make a list of interesting jobs. How many do you know? You have one minute.

**Lesson D  Guess!** Describe your favorite celebrity, but don't say his or her name! Can your partner guess the name? Take turns. You have two minutes.

A: *He's a singer and a musician. He's from England. He's in Coldplay.*
B: *Is he Chris Martin?*
A: *Yes!*

## 2 In the real world

What is your favorite movie? Go online and find information in English about five actors or actresses in the movie. Then write about them.

- What are their names?
- Where are they from?

> *Actors in "Star Wars"*
> *My favorite movie is "Star Wars."*
> *Harrison Ford is an actor in the movie.*
> *He's from the United States . . .*

# People and places

## Warm-up

Cdaana
*Canada*

Rsaius

Feracn

Moicex

Cahin

Bzarli

Shuto Aarfci

Asaiturla

**A** Write the names of the countries.

**B** Say the names of five other countries in English.

# A  *Where are you from?*

## 1 Vocabulary Nationalities

**A** 🔊 Complete the chart with the correct nationalities. Then listen and check your answers.

| | | | | | |
|---|---|---|---|---|---|
| Mexican | American | South Korean | Chilean | Greek | Colombian |
| Spanish | Canadian | Brazilian | Saudi | Peruvian | Japanese |
| British | Chinese | Turkish | Thai | Ecuadorian | ✓Australian |

| | Country | Nationality | | Country | Nationality |
|---|---|---|---|---|---|
| | Australia | *Australian* | | Japan | |
| | Brazil | | | Mexico | |
| | Britain | | | Peru | |
| | Canada | | | Saudi Arabia | |
| | Chile | | | South Korea | |
| | China | | | Spain | |
| | Colombia | | | Thailand | |
| | Ecuador | | | Turkey | |
| | Greece | | | the United States | |

**B Pair work** Say a famous name. Your partner says his or her nationality. Take turns.

> **A:** *Bill Gates.*
> **B:** *He's from the United States. He's American.*

## 2 Language in context New neighbors

🔊 Listen to Brad and Emily Hill talk about their new neighbors. What are their names?

**Brad:** Who are they?
**Emily:** Oh, they're our new neighbors, Carlos and Claudia.
**Brad:** Are they musicians?
**Emily:** Yes, they are.

**Brad:** Where are they from?
**Emily:** They're from Brazil.
**Brad:** What city are they from?
**Emily:** They're from Manaus.

16

# 3 Grammar  Plural subject pronouns; questions with *be*

| | |
|---|---|
| **Where** are you and Sakura from? | **Where** are Carlos and Claudia from? |
| **We're** from Japan. | **They're** from Brazil. |
| **What** city are **you** from? | **What** city are **they** from? |
| **We're** from Osaka. | **They're** from Manaus. |
| **Are you** Japanese? | **Are they** Brazilian? |
| Yes, **we are**. | Yes, **they are**. |
| No, **we're not**. / No, **we aren't**. | No, **they're not**. / No, **they aren't**. |

*Contractions*  we're = we are        they're = they are

Complete the conversations with the correct words.
Then practice with a partner.

1. **A:** Where are _____*you*_____ from?
   **B:** We're from Mexico.
   **A:** Oh? _____ city are you from? Are you from Mexico City?
   **B:** No, we _____ not. _____ from Monterrey.

2. **A:** _____ Jim and Carly American?
   **B:** No, they _____ . They _____ Canadian.
   **A:** What city in Canada are _____ from?
   **B:** They _____ from Toronto.

# 4 Pronunciation  Word stress

**A** ◀)) Listen and repeat. Notice the stressed syllables in the nationalities.

| ● | ●• | •●• | •● |
|---|---|---|---|
| **Greek** | **Bri**tish | Bra**zil**ian | Chi**nese** |

**B** ◀)) Listen. Underline the stressed syllable in each nationality.

Japa<u>nese</u>    Australian    Spanish    Thai

# 5 Speaking  That's not correct!

**A** Write three false sentences about people, countries, or nationalities.

**B Group work** Share your sentences. Your group corrects them. Take turns.

    **A:** *Toronto and Vancouver are in Greece.*
    **B:** *No, they aren't. They're in Canada.*

*1. Toronto and Vancouver are in Greece.*
*2. Venus and Serena Williams are Ecuadorian.*
*3. Nicole Kidman and Russell Crowe are British.*

# 6 Keep talking!

Go to page **127** for more practice.

I can ask for and say people's nationalities.

# 1 Numbers 0 to 10; phone numbers; email addresses

**A** 🔊 Listen and repeat.

| 0 zero | 1 one | 2 two | 3 three | 4 four | 5 five | 6 six | 7 seven | 8 eight | 9 nine | 10 ten |

**B** 🔊 Listen and repeat. Notice that people sometimes say "oh" for "zero" in phone numbers.

281-363-2301 = "two-eight-one, three-six-three, two-three-zero-one"

602-374-4188 = "six-oh-two, three-seven-four, four-one-eight-eight"

**C** 🔊 Listen and repeat. Notice the way people say email addresses.

susan8k@cup.org = "susan-eight-K-at-C-U-P-dot-org"

jun_akita@email.com = "jun-underscore-akita-at-email-dot-com"

# 2 Interactions    Phone numbers and email addresses

**A** 🔊 Listen and practice.

**Stacy:** Hey, Emma. What's your phone number?
**Emma:** It's 309-403-8708.
**Stacy:** What's your email address?
**Emma:** It's emma@cup.org.
**Stacy:** Thanks!

**B** 🔊 Listen to the expressions. Then practice the conversation again with the new expressions.

**Asking for someone's phone number**

What's your phone number?
What's your number?

**Asking for someone's email address**

What's your email address?
What's your email?

**C Pair work** Practice the conversation again with the information below.

978-887-8045      ej5@cup.org

604-608-4864      emma_jones@email.com

# 3 Listening What name, please?

**A** 🔊 Listen to four people call Directory Assistance for phone numbers.
Check (✓) the correct answers.

1. Carlos Moreno    ☐ 333-822-1607    ✓ 323-822-1607
2. Lucy Chang    ☐ 662-651-0410    ☐ 662-615-0410
3. Michael Ashcroft    ☐ 866-279-9400    ☐ 866-279-9500
4. Beatriz J. Lago    ☐ 341-360-7450    ☐ 341-360-4570

**B** 🔊 Listen to three people give their names, phone numbers, and email addresses.
Complete the forms.

**MADISON ENGLISH SCHOOL**

**REGISTRATION**

First name: _____Michael_____

Middle name: _____John_____

Last name: _____

Phone: _____

Email: _____

**1-2-3 GYM**

**MEMBERSHIP**

First name: _____

Middle initial: _____P._____

Last name: _____

Phone: _____

Email: _____

**City Library**

**CARD APPLICATION**

First name: _____

Family name: _____

City: _____Dallas_____

Phone: _____

Email: _____

# 4 Speaking A new number and email address

**A** Write a new phone number and email address.

My new phone number: _____    My new email address: _____

**B Class activity** Ask five classmates for their names, new phone numbers, and
new email addresses. Complete the chart with their answers.

| | Name | Phone number | Email address |
|---|---|---|---|
| 1. | | | |
| 2. | | | |
| 3. | | | |
| 4. | | | |
| 5. | | | |

**C** Share your information.

   **A:** *What's her name and phone number?*
   **B:** *Her name is Fatima. Her phone number is 212-691-3239.*
   **A:** *What's her email address?*
   **B:** *Her email is . . .*

> *I can* ask for and give phone numbers and email addresses. ☑

# Family

## 1 Vocabulary Family members

**A** Listen and repeat.

grandmother
Sarah Mills

grandfather
Roger Mills

grandparents

mother (mom)
Helen Olson

father (dad)
Michael Olson

parents

children / kids

wife | husband

daughter | son

brother
Jack Olson

sister
Wendy Olson

brother
Brian Olson

**B Pair work** Ask and answer the questions about the family in Part A.

1. Are Sarah and Roger Mills single?
2. Are Michael and Helen brother and sister?
3. Are Sarah and Roger grandparents?
4. Are Wendy and Jack parents?

## 2 Conversation Who's that?

Listen and practice.

**Lance:** Who's that?
**Jack:** That's my sister. Her name is Wendy.
**Lance:** How old is she?
**Jack:** She's seven.
**Lance:** Is she your only sister?
**Jack:** Yeah.
**Lance:** And who are they?
**Jack:** They're my grandparents.
**Lance:** Wow. They look young.
And who's he?
**Jack:** That's me!

# 3 Grammar 🔊   *Who* and *How old* with *be*

**Who's** that?
  That's my sister.
**How old is** she?
  She's seven (years old).

**Who are** they?
  They're my grandparents.
**How old are** they?
  They're 70 and 66.

🔊 **Numbers 11–101**

| | |
|---|---|
| **11** | eleven |
| **12** | twelve |
| **13** | thirteen |
| **14** | fourteen |
| **15** | fifteen |
| **16** | sixteen |
| **17** | seventeen |
| **18** | eighteen |
| **19** | nineteen |
| **20** | twenty |
| **21** | twenty-one |
| **22** | twenty-two |
| **23** | twenty-three |
| **24** | twenty-four |
| **25** | twenty-five |
| **26** | twenty-six |
| **27** | twenty-seven |
| **28** | twenty-eight |
| **29** | twenty-nine |
| **30** | thirty |
| **40** | forty |
| **50** | fifty |
| **60** | sixty |
| **70** | seventy |
| **80** | eighty |
| **90** | ninety |
| **100** | one hundred |
| **101** | one hundred (and) one |

**A** Read the answers. Write the questions. Then practice with a partner.

A: *Who's that?* _____
B: Oh, that's my brother Ignacio.
A: _____
B: He's ten years old.
A: _____
B: They're my sisters Lucia, Antonia, and Carmen.
A: _____
B: They're 19, 16, and 11.
A: And _____
B: That's my grandfather.
A: _____
B: He's 62.

**B Pair work** Ask and answer questions about the family in Exercise 1.

A: *Who's that?*
B: *That's Jack Olson.*

# 4 Speaking  My family

**A** Complete the chart with information about three people in your family.

| | Family member | Name | How old . . . ? | Where . . . from? |
|---|---|---|---|---|
| 1. | | | | |
| 2. | | | | |
| 3. | | | | |

**B Pair work** Tell your partner about your family. Ask and answer questions for more information.

A: *Keiko is my grandmother. She's 73.*
B: *Where is she from?*

# 5 Keep talking!

Go to page 129 for more practice.

*I can* identify family members and give their ages. ☑

# D Family and friends

## 1 Reading 🔊

**A** Look at the people in Isabel's photos. Who are they? Guess.

**B** Read the photo descriptions. Who are Isabel's family members? Who are her friends?

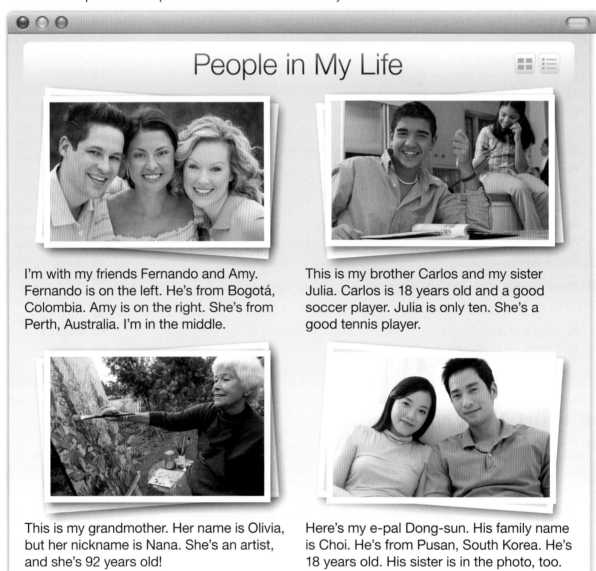

## People in My Life

I'm with my friends Fernando and Amy. Fernando is on the left. He's from Bogotá, Colombia. Amy is on the right. She's from Perth, Australia. I'm in the middle.

This is my brother Carlos and my sister Julia. Carlos is 18 years old and a good soccer player. Julia is only ten. She's a good tennis player.

This is my grandmother. Her name is Olivia, but her nickname is Nana. She's an artist, and she's 92 years old!

Here's my e-pal Dong-sun. His family name is Choi. He's from Pusan, South Korea. He's 18 years old. His sister is in the photo, too.

**C** Read the photo descriptions again. Correct the false sentences.

1. Isabel and Amy are ~~sisters.~~          _Isabel and Amy are friends._
2. Carlos isn't a good soccer player.     _____
3. Olivia is 90 years old.                _____
4. Isabel and Dong-sun are classmates.    _____

**D Pair work** Ask and answer the questions about Isabel's family and friends.

- Who are Fernando and Amy?
- What's Olivia's nickname?
- How old is Julia?
- What city is Dong-sun from?

## 2 **Listening** People I know

**A** ◀)) Listen to Gina show some photos to her friend. Who are the people?
Check (✓) the correct answers.

1. ☐ friend
   ✓ brother

2. ☐ classmate
   ☐ sister

3. ☐ father
   ☐ grandfather

4. ☐ teacher
   ☐ mother

**B** ◀)) Listen again. Answer the questions.

1. How old is Mark? _____ *15* _____
2. What city is Dominique from? _____
3. What's the man's name? _____
4. Is Ms. Parker American? _____

## 3 **Writing and speaking** My friends

**A** Complete the chart with information about three friends. Then find photos or draw pictures of them.

|  | Friend 1 | Friend 2 | Friend 3 |
|---|---|---|---|
| Name |  |  |  |
| Age |  |  |  |
| Nationality |  |  |  |
| Other information |  |  |  |

**B** Write sentences about your friends in the pictures. Use the model and your answers in Part A to help you.

> ### My Friends
> My best friend is Samantha. She's 26 years old.
> She's American. She's a teacher.
>     Jill is my friend, too. She's . . .

**C Group work** Share your pictures and sentences. Ask and answer questions for more information.

> A: *This is my friend Samantha. She's 26 years old.*
> B: *What's her last name?*

*I can give information about family and friends.* ☑

# Wrap-up

## 1 Quick pair review

**Lesson A  Guess!** Say five countries. Can your partner name the nationalities? Take turns. You have two minutes.

**A:** *South Korea.*
**B:** *South Korean.*

**Lesson B  Test your partner!** Write three phone numbers and say them to your partner. Can your partner write them correctly? Check his or her answers. You have two minutes.

| My phone numbers | My partner's phone numbers |
| --- | --- |
| _____ | _____ |
| _____ | _____ |
| _____ | _____ |

**Lesson C  Brainstorm!** Make a list of family words. How many do you know? You have one minute.

**Lesson D  Find out!** Are any of your friends or family members from the same cities? You have two minutes.

**A:** *My father is from Mexico City, and my mother is from Guadalajara.*
**B:** *My grandmother is from Guadalajara, too!*

## 2 In the real world

Go online and find information in English about a country from another part of the world. Then write about it.

- What are five cities in the country?
- What are the names and ages of two famous people from the country?

> *French Cities and People*
> *Paris, Bordeaux, Cannes, Lyon, and Dijon*
> *are five cities in France. Marion Cotillard is*
> *a famous actress from France. She's . . .*

# What's that?

## Warm-up

Year: <u>*1969*</u>

Year: _____

Year: _____

Year: _____

**A** Label the pictures with the correct years.

✓1969    1978    1986    1994

**B** Can you name five things in the pictures?

# A Is this your notebook?

## 1 Vocabulary Everyday items

**A** ◀)) Listen and repeat.

☐ a bag      ☐ a book      ☐ a cell phone      ☐ a dictionary

☐ an eraser      ☐ a key      ☐ a laptop      ☐ a notebook

☐ a pen      ☐ sunglasses      ☐ an umbrella      ☐ a watch

**B Pair work** Check (✓) the things in your classroom. Then compare answers.

## 2 Language in context What are those?

◀)) Listen to four people talk about everyday items. Circle the items in the conversations.

Pete: Hey, Ling. What's that?
Ling: Oh, it's my dictionary.
Pete: It's nice. What are those?
Ling: They're my English books.

Susie: Are these your sunglasses?
Kyle: No, they're not.
Susie: Is this your notebook?
Kyle: Yes, it is. Thanks.

# 3 Grammar  Demonstratives; articles *a* and *an*; plurals

What's **this**?    What's **that**?

It's my dictionary.
Is **this** your dictionary?
Is **that** your dictionary?
    Yes, **it is**.    No, **it's not**.

What are **these**?    What are **those**?

**They're** my English books.
Are **these** your English books?
Are **those** your English books?
    Yes, **they are**.    No, **they're not**.

*Articles* a *and* an
**a** + consonant sound    **a b**ag
**an** + vowel sound    **an e**raser

*Plurals*
a book → two book**s**
a watch → two watch**es**
a dictionary → two dictionar**ies**
Note: *Sunglasses* and *glasses* are always plural.

**A** Complete the conversations with the correct words. Then practice with a partner.

A: What*'s this*____? 
B: *It's a watch.*____

A: What _____? 
B: _____

A: What _____? 
B: _____

A: What _____? 
B: _____

**B** **Pair work** Ask and answer questions about everyday items in your classroom.

# 4 Pronunciation Plurals

 Listen and repeat. Notice that some words have an extra syllable in their plural forms.

| Same syllables | Extra syllables |
|---|---|
| eraser / erasers | actress / actress·es |
| key / keys | address / address·es |
| laptop / laptops | watch / watch·es |

# 5 Speaking In my bag

**Pair work** Ask and answer 10 questions about the everyday items in your bags and in the classroom.

A: *Is this your English book?*
B: *No, it's not. It's my dictionary. What are those?*
A: *They're my keys.*

# 6 Keep talking!

Go to page 130 for more practice.

I can ask about and identify everyday items. ✓

# B What's this called in English?

## 1 Listening Around the classroom

**A** 🔊 Listen to Bo and Marta ask about new words in English. Number the pictures from 1 to 5.

☐ an alarm clock  ☐ a map  ☐ a marker  ☐ a poster  1 a remote control

**B** What things in Part A are in your classroom?

## 2 Interactions  Asking about new words

**A** 🔊 Listen and practice.

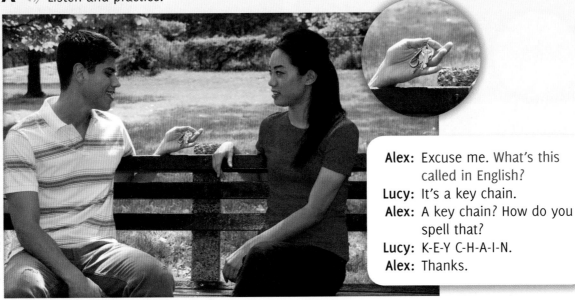

**Alex:** Excuse me. What's this called in English?
**Lucy:** It's a key chain.
**Alex:** A key chain? How do you spell that?
**Lucy:** K-E-Y C-H-A-I-N.
**Alex:** Thanks.

**B** 🔊 Listen to the expressions. Then practice the conversation again with the new expressions.

### Asking what something is

What's this called in English?
What's the word for this in English?
How do you say this in English?

**C Pair work** Practice the conversation again with the things in Exercise 1.

A: *Excuse me. What's this called in English?*
B: *It's a map.*
A: *How do you spell that?*

# 3 **Speaking** More everyday items

**A** 🔊)) Listen and repeat.

1. a camera
2. a flash drive
3. a hairbrush
4. a newspaper
5. a magazine
6. a comb
7. a coin
8. a wallet

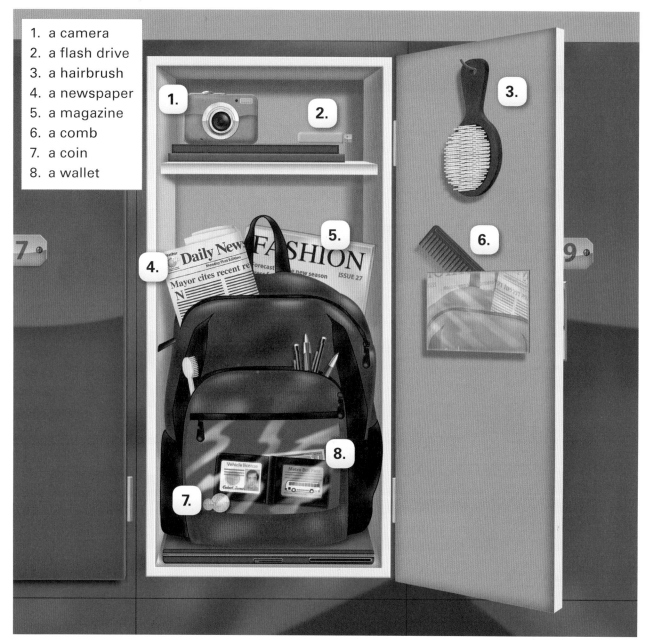

**B** **Pair work** Cover the words. What is each thing called? Answer with the information you remember.

A: *What's this called?*
B: *I think it's a . . .*

**C** **Pair work** Ask and answer questions about other things in the picture.

A: *What's the word for this in English?*
B: *It's a student I.D.*
A: *What's this called?*
B: *Hmm . . . I don't know. Let's ask the teacher.*

**I can** *ask what something is called in English.* ☑

# **C** *Clothing*

## **1 Vocabulary** Clothes and colors

**A** 🔊 Listen and repeat.

| Clothes | | Colors |
|---|---|---|
| Ana | Greg | red |
| | | pink |
| sweatshirt / hat | coat | orange |
| dress | scarf | yellow |
| blouse | jacket | green |
| | tie / T-shirt | blue |
| jeans | suit | purple |
| sweater | | black |
| skirt | shorts | brown |
| belt | shirt / shoes | white |
| boots | pants / socks | gray |

**B Pair work** Describe a classmate's clothes, but don't say his or her name!
Your partner guesses the name. Take turns.

> **A:** *His shoes are brown. His T-shirt is red and green. His pants are gray.*
> **B:** *Is it David?*

## **2 Conversation** Whose bag is it?

🔊 Listen and practice.

**Greg:** Excuse me. I think that's my bag.
**Laura:** This bag?
**Greg:** Yes. I think it's mine.
**Laura:** It is? Oh, yes. This bag is black and yellow.
 Mine is black and green. I'm very sorry.
**Greg:** That's OK. Is that bag yours?
**Laura:** Yes, thank you.
**Greg:** You're welcome.

## 3 Grammar 🔊 Possessive pronouns; *Whose*; *'s and s'*

It's my bag. → It's **mine**.
It's your jacket. → It's **yours**.
It's his coat. → It's **his**.
They're her shoes. → They're **hers**.
They're our clothes. → They're **ours**.
It's their bag. → It's **theirs**.

**Whose** bag is this?
   It's Greg**'s** (bag).
**Whose** bag is that?
   It's the student**'s** (bag).
**Whose** bags are those?
   They're the student**s'** (bags).

**A** Circle the correct words. Then practice with a partner.

1. Whose clothes are these?     They're **your** / **our** / **ours**.
2. Are these Greg's black shoes?     Yes, they're **his** / **hers** / **theirs**.
3. Is this pink scarf Ana's?     No, it's not **his** / **hers** / **theirs**.
4. Are these bags Greg and Ana's?     Yes, they're **his** / **hers** / **theirs**.
5. Whose red socks are these? Are they yours?     Yes, they're **my** / **mine** / **yours**.
6. Is that my sister's skirt?     No, it's not **mine** / **yours** / **hers**.

**B Pair work** Ask and answer questions about the clothing in Exercise 1.

A: *Whose jeans are these?*
B: *They're Ana's. Whose T-shirt is this?*
A: *It's . . .*

## 4 Speaking   Yes, it's mine.

**Class activity** Put three of your things on a table. Then take three other things and find their owners.

A: *Whose scarf is this?*
B: *I think it's Mary's.*
A: *Is this your scarf, Mary?*
C: *Yes, it's mine.*

## 5 Keep talking!

Student A go to page **131** and Student B go to page **132** for more practice.

*I can talk about clothes and possessions.* ☑

# D Favorite things

## 1 Reading 🔊

**A** Look at the pictures. What clothes and colors are they?

**B** Read the webpage. What countries are the people from?

## What's your favorite item of clothing?

SEND US YOUR PICTURES!

This cap is my favorite. It's from my baseball team. Our team colors are blue and white.

*– Joe, the U.S.*

These boots are my favorite. I think they're from the 1970s. They're red. Red is my favorite color!

*– Ariela, Venezuela*

Here's a photo of my favorite pants. They're called *salwar*. These are men's pants, and they're from India.

*– Sadi, Canada*

This dress is my favorite item of clothing. It's called a *hanbok* in Korean. It's my mother's.

*– Bin-woo, South Korea*

Here's my favorite item of clothing. It's an old shirt. It's from London in the 1980s.

*– Ian, the U.K.*

This scarf is my favorite item of clothing. It's from Thailand. The blue color is nice.

*– Mariko, Japan*

**C** Read the webpage again. Answer the questions.

1. What's Joe's favorite thing? _His favorite thing is a baseball cap._

2. What is Ariela's favorite color? _____

3. What are Sadi's pants called? _____

4. What's Bin-woo's favorite item of clothing? _____

5. Where is Ian's shirt from? _____

6. Where is Mariko's scarf from? _____

**D Pair work** What's your favorite item of clothing? Tell your partner.

*"My favorite item of clothing is my blue sweatshirt."*

## 2 Listening It's my favorite.

🔊 Listen to four people talk about their favorite things. Check (✓) the things they describe.

1.
a. ✓
b. ☐

2.
a. ☐
b. ☐

3.
a. ☐
b. ☐

4.
a. ☐
b. ☐

## 3 Writing and speaking My favorite thing

**A** Draw a picture of your favorite thing. Then answer the questions.

- What is it? _____
- Where is it from? _____
- How old is it? _____
- What color is it? _____

**B** Write about your favorite thing. Use the model and your answers in Part A to help you.

> *My Favorite Thing*
> *My favorite thing is my bag. It's from Cuzco, Peru. I think it's three or four years old. It's purple, white, and yellow. I love it!*

**C Group work** Share your drawings and your writing. Ask and answer questions for more information.

**A:** *Here's a picture of my favorite thing.*
**B:** *What is it?*
**A:** *It's my bag.*
**C:** *Where is it from?*
**A:** *It's from Peru.*

I can *describe my favorite possessions.* ☑

# Wrap-up

## 1 Quick pair review

**Lesson A Brainstorm!** Make a list of everyday items and the plural forms of the words. How many do you know? You have two minutes.

**Lesson B Test your partner!** Ask your partner what the things are. You have two minutes.

**Student A**

**Student B**

**Lesson C Do you remember?** Look at your partner's clothes. Then close your eyes and describe them. Take turns. You have two minutes.

*"Your shirt is green, and your jeans are blue. I think your socks are white."*

**Lesson D Find out!** What is one thing both you and your partner have in your bags or desks? Find the thing and answer the questions. You have two minutes.

- What color is it?
- How old is it?
- Where is it from?

## 2 In the real world

What's in style? Find a picture of clothes in a magazine. Then write about them.

- What clothes are in the picture?
- What colors are the clothes?

> *Clothes in "Style Today"*
> *The woman's sweater in the picture is blue. Her pants are brown, and her shoes are black. Her bag is . . .*

# Daily life

| LESSON **A** | LESSON **B** | LESSON **C** | LESSON **D** |
|---|---|---|---|
| • Ways of getting around<br>• Simple present statements | • Asking the time | • Days of the week and routines<br>• Simple present *yes* / *no* questions | • Reading: "What's your favorite day of the week?"<br>• Writing: About my weekend |

# Warm-up

**A** Name the things you see in the picture. Use *That's a / an* . . . and *Those are* . . . .

**B** Say the colors of six things in the picture.

# A Getting around

## 1 Vocabulary Ways of getting around

**A** 🔊 Listen and repeat.

drive a car

ride a bicycle / bike

ride a motorcycle

take a taxi / cab

take the bus

take the subway

take the train

walk

**B** 🔊 Listen to five ways of getting around. Number them from 1 to 5.

☐ a bicycle    ☐ 1 a bus    ☐ a car    ☐ a motorcycle    ☐ a train

## 2 Language in context Going to work and school

**A** 🔊 Listen to Mariela describe how she and her family get to work and school. Underline the ways they get around.

I have a car. I <u>drive</u> to work. I don't take the train.

My husband doesn't drive to work. He has a bike, so he rides his bike.

My kids walk to school. They don't take the bus.

**B** What about you? Check (✓) the ways you get around.

☐ I drive.    ☐ I take the bus.    ☐ I ride a bike.    ☐ I walk.

## 3 Grammar 🔊  Simple present statements

| Regular verbs | | Irregular verbs | |
| --- | --- | --- | --- |

**Regular verbs**

I **drive** to work.
You **take** a taxi.
He **rides** a bike.
She **drives**.
We **take** the train.
They **walk** to school.

I **don't take** the train.
You **don't take** the subway.
He **doesn't drive** to work.
She **doesn't walk**.
We **don't take** a taxi.
They **don't take** the bus.

**Irregular verbs**

| I / you / we / they | he / she / it |
| --- | --- |
| I **have** a car. | She **has** a car. |
| You **don't have** a bike. | She **doesn't have** a bike. |
| We **go** to work. | He **goes** to work. |
| They **don't go** to school. | He **doesn't go** to school. |

*Contractions*  don't = do not    doesn't = does not

**A** Complete the sentences with the simple present forms of the verbs. Then compare with a partner.

1. I ___take___ (take) the bus to school. I ___don't walk___ (not / walk).
2. Jonathan _____ (have) a car. He _____ (drive) to work.
3. My parents _____ (take) the train to work. They _____ (go) to the city.
4. My neighbor _____ (ride) a motorcycle to work.
5. Mei-li _____ (not / take) the bus. She _____ (walk).
6. We _____ (not / have) bicycles, and we _____ (not / drive).

**B Pair work** Make five sentences about how your family members and friends get to school or work. Tell your partner.

A: *My sister works in a big city. She takes the bus to work.*
B: *My best friend works in a big city, too. He doesn't take the bus. He drives.*

## 4 Speaking  I take the bus.

**A** Write how you get to school or work in the chart. Add extra information, such as a bus number or a train number.

| | Me | Name: _____ | Name: _____ | Name: _____ |
| --- | --- | --- | --- | --- |
| To school | | | | |
| To work | | | | |
| Extra information | | | | |

**B Group work** Find out how three of your classmates get to school or work. Complete the chart with their information.

A: *I take the bus to school. It's the number 16 bus. How about you?*
B: *I take the bus, too. I take the number 8 bus.*

**C Group work** Tell another group how your classmates get to school or work.

"*Daniel takes the number 8 bus to school.*"

## 5 Keep talking!

Go to page 133 for more practice.

*I can describe how people get around.* ✓

37

# B What time is it?

## 1 Telling time

**A** 🔊 Listen and repeat.

It's twelve o'clock.

It's noon.
It's twelve p.m.

It's midnight.
It's twelve a.m.

It's twelve-oh-five.
It's five after twelve.

It's twelve-fifteen.
It's a quarter after twelve.

It's twelve-thirty.
It's half past twelve.

It's twelve-forty.
It's twenty to one.

It's twelve forty-five.
It's a quarter to one.

**B Pair work** Say the times in two ways.

9:45    7:30    6:03    1:15    11:40

a.m. = midnight to noon
p.m. = noon to midnight

## 2 Interactions    Time

**A** 🔊 Listen and practice.

**Joe:** What time is it?
**Mike:** It's 9:15. What time is the bus?
**Joe:** Nine-twenty. We're early.

**Keisha:** What's the time?
**Emily:** It's 9:35. What time is our class?
**Keisha:** It's at 9:30. We're late!

### Asking the time

What time is it?
What's the time?

**B Pair work** Practice the conversations again with the times below.

4:15 / 4:45    6:20 / 7:00    10:05 / 10:00    5:45 / 5:30

## 3 **Pronunciation** Reduction of *to*

**A** 🔊 Listen and repeat. Notice how *to* is pronounced as /tə/.

/tə/         /tə/         /tə/

It's ten to five.     It's five to two.     It's a quarter to one.

**B** 🔊 Listen to the conversations. Then practice them. Reduce *to* to /tə/.

**A:** *Is it five to one?*     **A:** *Is it ten to eight?*     **A:** *Is it a quarter to three?*
**B:** *No, it's ten to one.*     **B:** *No, it's a quarter to eight.*     **B:** *No, it's twenty to three.*

## 4 **Listening** Am I late?

**A** 🔊 Listen to five conversations about time. Write the time of each thing.

1. the movie    2. Rod's class    3. the train    4. the bus    5. Susan's class
    _10:00_      _____      _____      _____      _____

**B** 🔊 Listen again. Are the people early or late? Circle the correct answers.

1. (early)/ late    2. early / late    3. early / late    4. early / late    5. early / late

## 5 **Speaking** What time is . . . ?

**A Pair work** Interview your partner. Take notes.

**What time is your . . . ?**

favorite class         lunch break         favorite TV show

_____     _____     _____

**A:** *What time is your favorite class?*
**B:** *It's at 7:30 a.m. What time is yours?*
**A:** *Mine is at 8:00 p.m. It's this class!*

**B Pair work** Tell another classmate about your partner's answers.

*"Ji-sung's favorite class is at 7:30 a.m."*

I can **ask for and tell the time.** ☑

# C My routine

## 1 Vocabulary Days of the week and routines

**A** 🔊 Listen and repeat.

| Weekdays | | | | | The weekend | |
|----------|---------|-----------|----------|--------|-------------|--------|
| Monday | Tuesday | Wednesday | Thursday | Friday | Saturday | Sunday |

**B** 🔊 Listen and repeat.

get up    drink coffee    eat breakfast    read the news    go to school

exercise    cook dinner    study    watch TV    go to bed

**C Pair work** What is your routine on weekdays? on weekends? Tell your partner.

*"I get up and eat breakfast on weekdays. I go to school. I study . . ."*

## 2 Conversation Monday morning

🔊 Listen and practice.

**Tom:** It's Monday morning . . . again!
 **Liz:** Do you get up early on weekdays?
**Tom:** Yes, I do. I get up at 5:30 a.m.
 **Liz:** Wow! That *is* early!
**Tom:** And I study all morning and afternoon.
 **Liz:** Do you study in the evenings, too?
**Tom:** No, I don't. I cook dinner, exercise, and go to bed late, after midnight.
 **Liz:** That's not good. What about on weekends?
**Tom:** On weekends, I sleep!

# 3 Grammar 🔊 | Simple present *yes* / *no* questions

**Do** you **go** to school on Mondays?
    Yes, I **do**.    No, I **don't**.

**Does** Liz **exercise**?
    Yes, she **does**.    No, she **doesn't**.

**Do** you and your friends **watch** TV?
    Yes, we **do**.    No, we **don't**.

**Do** your friends **study**?
    Yes, they **do**.    No, they **don't**.

**A** Write *yes* / *no* questions with the information below. Then compare with a partner.

1. (you / get up / 7:00)     *Do you get up at 7:00?*
2. (you / read the news / every day)   _____
3. (your teacher / drink coffee / in class)   _____
4. (your parents / watch TV / in the evening)   _____
5. (your friend / exercise / on weekends)   _____
6. (you and your friends / study / after midnight)   _____

**B Pair work** Ask and answer the questions in Part A. Answer with your own information.

> A: *Do you get up at 7:00?*
> B: *No, I don't. I get up at 6:00 on weekdays and 9:30 on weekends.*

# 4 Speaking Routines

**A Pair work** Interview your partner. Check (✓) his or her answers.

| Do you . . . ? | Yes | No |
|---|---|---|
| cook dinner on weekends | ☐ | ☐ |
| drink coffee after 7:00 p.m. | ☐ | ☐ |
| exercise every day | ☐ | ☐ |
| go to bed late on weekdays | ☐ | ☐ |
| get up early on weekdays | ☐ | ☐ |
| read the news in the evening | ☐ | ☐ |

> A: *Do you cook dinner on weekends?*
> B: *No, I don't. I cook on weekdays!*

**B Pair work** Tell another classmate about your partner's routines.

> A: *Does Rita cook dinner on weekends?*
> B: *No, she doesn't. She cooks on weekdays!*

🔊 **Time expressions**

on Sunday(s)
on Sunday afternoon(s)
on weekdays
on the weekend
on weekends
in the morning(s)
in the afternoon(s)
in the evening(s)
at noon / midnight
at night
before 7:00
after midnight
every day

# 5 Keep talking!

Go to page 134 for more practice.

*I can* ask and answer questions about routines. ☑

# D My weekend

## 1 Reading 🔊

**A** Look at the message board question. What's *your* favorite day of the week? Why?

**B** Read the message board. Whose favorite day is on the weekend?

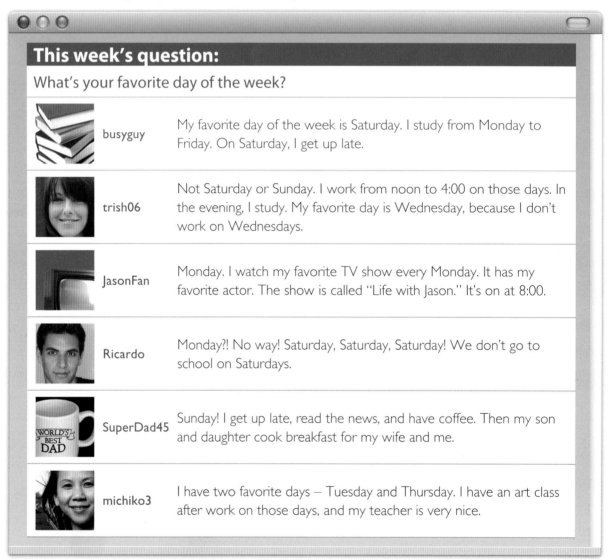

**This week's question:**

What's your favorite day of the week?

| | | |
|---|---|---|
| | busyguy | My favorite day of the week is Saturday. I study from Monday to Friday. On Saturday, I get up late. |
| | trish06 | Not Saturday or Sunday. I work from noon to 4:00 on those days. In the evening, I study. My favorite day is Wednesday, because I don't work on Wednesdays. |
| | JasonFan | Monday. I watch my favorite TV show every Monday. It has my favorite actor. The show is called "Life with Jason." It's on at 8:00. |
| | Ricardo | Monday?! No way! Saturday, Saturday, Saturday! We don't go to school on Saturdays. |
| | SuperDad45 | Sunday! I get up late, read the news, and have coffee. Then my son and daughter cook breakfast for my wife and me. |
| | michiko3 | I have two favorite days – Tuesday and Thursday. I have an art class after work on those days, and my teacher is very nice. |

**C** Read the message board again. What's each person's favorite day? Why?
Complete the chart.

| | Favorite day(s) | Why? |
|---|---|---|
| 1. busyguy | *Saturday* | *gets up late* |
| 2. trish06 | | |
| 3. JasonFan | | |
| 4. Ricardo | | |
| 5. SuperDad45 | | |
| 6. michiko3 | | |

**D Class activity** What's your class's favorite day? Vote and discuss your answer.

## 2 Listening Angela's routine

**A** 🔊 Listen to Angela talk about her routine on weekends. Circle the activities she does.

| Saturdays | | Sundays | |
|---|---|---|---|
| (work) | watch TV | get up late | exercise |
| go to class | go to bed late | study | cook |

**B** 🔊 Listen again. Write one more thing Angela does on Saturdays and on Sundays.

On Saturdays: _____    On Sundays: _____

## 3 Writing About my weekend

**A** Complete the chart with information about your weekend routine. Include two activities you do and two activities you don't do.

**Saturdays**                      **Sundays**

Activities I do:                   Activities I do:

• _____              • _____

• _____              • _____

Activities I don't do:             Activities I don't do:

• _____              • _____

• _____              • _____

*My Weekend Routine*
*On Saturdays, I get up late and watch TV. I don't study, and I don't go to work. On Sundays, . . .*

**B** Write about your weekend routine. Use the model and your answers in Part A to help you.

**C** Group work Share your writing. Ask and answer questions for more information.

## 4 Speaking Are you busy?

**A** Add two questions about routines to the survey. Then circle your answers.

| ARE YOU BUSY? | Me | | You | |
|---|---|---|---|---|
| 1. Do you study English every weekend? | Yes | No | Yes | No |
| 2. Do you go to work on the weekend? | Yes | No | Yes | No |
| 3. Do you get up before 7:00 on the weekend? | Yes | No | Yes | No |
| 4. Do you exercise on the weekend? | Yes | No | Yes | No |
| 5. | Yes | No | Yes | No |
| 6. | Yes | No | Yes | No |

**B** Pair work Interview your partner. Circle his or her answers. Is your partner busy?

*I can describe the things I do on weekends.* ☑

# Wrap-up

## 1 Quick pair review

**Lesson A  Brainstorm!** Make a list of ways of getting around. How many do you know? You have one minute.

**Lesson B  Test your partner!** Say four different times. Can your partner write them correctly? Check his or her answers. You have two minutes.

**Lesson C  Guess!** Say a time and a day. Can your partner guess your routine at that time? Take turns. You have two minutes.

**A:** *Two o'clock on Monday.*
**B:** *Do you exercise at 2:00 on Monday?*
**A:** *No.*
**B:** *Do you study?*
**A:** *Yes.*

**Lesson D  Find out!** What are three things both you and your partner do on weekends? You have two minutes.

**A:** *I exercise on Saturday mornings. How about you?*
**B:** *No, I don't. I go to bed late on Saturdays. How about you?*
**A:** *Yes, I do!*

## 2 In the real world

What time is it around the world? Go online and find the local time in these cities.

| Beijing | Cairo | Los Angeles | Rio de Janeiro | Tokyo |
|---|---|---|---|---|
| Buenos Aires | London | Mexico City | Sydney | Toronto |

*What time is it now?*
*It is nine o'clock in the evening in Beijing now. In Buenos Aires, it's . . .*

# Free time

# Warm-up

**A** Look at the pictures. Make two sentences about each one.

**B** When do you have free time? Write the times.

|  | Monday | Tuesday | Wednesday | Thursday | Friday | Saturday | Sunday |
|---|---|---|---|---|---|---|---|
| a.m. |  |  |  |  |  |  |  |
| p.m. |  |  |  |  |  |  |  |

**A** *Online habits*

## 1 Vocabulary Online activities

**A** 🔊 Listen and repeat.

☐ chat with friends

☐ check email

☐ download music

☐ play games

☐ post comments

☐ search the Internet

☐ shop online

☐ upload videos

**B Pair work** Check (✓) the things you do online. Then tell your partner.

*"I download music, post comments, and play games. How about you?"*

## 2 Language in context Habits survey

**A** 🔊 Read the survey about online habits. Circle the online activities.

### Habits survey

**1.** Do you ever (shop online)?
- ✓ Yes, I often shop online.
- ☐ Yes, I sometimes shop online.
- ☐ No, I never shop online.

**2.** Do you ever download music?
- ☐ Yes, I often download music.
- ✓ Yes, I sometimes download music.
- ☐ No, I never download music.

**3.** Do you ever post comments on blogs?
- ☐ Yes, I often post comments.
- ☐ Yes, I sometimes post comments.
- ✓ No, I never post comments.

**B** What about you? Do you do the online activities in the survey?

# 3 Grammar 🔊 Adverbs of frequency

| | | 100% | Do you **ever** shop online? |
|---|---|---|---|
| I | always usually often sometimes hardly ever never | shop online. | Yes, I sometimes shop online. / Yes, I sometimes do. No, I never shop online. / No, I never do. |
| | | 0% | |

**A** Rewrite the conversations with the adverbs of frequency. Then practice with a partner.

1. **A:** Do you download movies? (ever)      *Do you ever download movies?*
   **B:** Yes, I download movies. (often)   _____
2. **A:** Do you check email in class? (ever)  _____
   **B:** No, I check email in class. (never)  _____
3. **A:** Do you play games online? (ever)   _____
   **B:** Yes, I do. (usually)            _____
4. **A:** Do you post comments online? (ever)  _____
   **B:** No, I do that. (hardly ever)     _____

**B Pair work** Ask and answer the questions in Part A. Answer with your own information.

**A:** *Do you ever download movies?*
**B:** *Yes, I sometimes do.*

# 4 Speaking Often, sometimes, or never?

**A** Complete the chart with information about your online habits. Use the ideas in Exercise 1 and your own ideas.

| I often . . . | I sometimes . . . | I never . . . |
|---|---|---|
| • | • | • |
| • | • | • |

**B Group work** Compare your online habits.

**A:** *I often play games online.*
**B:** *Oh? I never do that.*
**C:** *I sometimes do.*

# 5 Keep talking!

Go to page 135 for more practice.

I can *talk about my online habits.*

47

# B How much is it?

## 1 Prices

**A** 🔊 Listen and repeat.

| | | |
|---|---|---|
| $79.00 | = | seventy-nine dollars |
| $79.95 | = | seventy-nine dollars and ninety-five cents |
| | OR | seventy-nine ninety-five |
| $379.95 | = | three hundred seventy-nine dollars and ninety-five cents |
| | OR | three seventy-nine ninety-five |

**B** 🔊 Listen and practice.

A: *How much is this?*　　A: *How much are these?*　　A: *How much is that watch?*
B: *It's $54.89.*　　　　　B: *They're $234.99.*　　　　B: *It's only $109.25.*

**C Pair work** Practice the conversations again. Say the prices in a different way.

## 2 Interactions　　At the store

**A** 🔊 Listen and practice.

Salesperson: Hello.
　　Margaret: Hi.
Salesperson: Can I help you?
　　Margaret: No, thanks. I'm just looking.

Salesperson: Can I help you?
　　Renato: Yes, please. How much is
　　　　　　 this camera?
Salesperson: It's $169.50.
　　Renato: Thanks.

**B** 🔊 Listen to the expressions. Then practice the conversations again with the new expressions.

| Declining help |
|---|
| No, thanks. I'm just looking. |
| No. I'm fine, thanks. |

| Accepting help |
|---|
| Yes, please. |
| Yes, thanks. |

## 3 Pronunciation Thirteen or thirty?

**A** 🔊 Listen and repeat. Notice the difference in stress in the numbers.

**B** 🔊 Listen to four conversations about prices. Circle the correct prices.

1. (\$14)/ \$40    3. \$17 / \$70
2. \$16 / \$60    4. \$19 / \$90

**C Pair work** Say a number from the chart. Your partner points to it. Take turns.

| Last syllable | First syllable |
|---|---|
| 13 thir**teen** | 30 **thir**ty |
| 14 four**teen** | 40 **for**ty |
| 15 fif**teen** | 50 **fif**ty |
| 16 six**teen** | 60 **six**ty |
| 17 seven**teen** | 70 **se**venty |
| 18 eigh**teen** | 80 **eigh**ty |
| 19 nine**teen** | 90 **nine**ty |

## 4 Listening Can I help you?

**A** 🔊 Listen to four conversations in a store. Check (✓) the words you hear.

1. ✓ camera
   ☐ cell phone
   ☐ laptop
2. ☐ shirts
   ☐ skirt
   ☐ T-shirt
3. ☐ bag
   ☐ bags
   ☐ belt
4. ☐ scarf
   ☐ shorts
   ☐ skirt

**B** 🔊 Listen to a salesperson offer help to four customers. Do the customers accept or decline help? Circle the correct answers.

1. (accept)/ decline    2. accept / decline    3. accept / decline    4. accept / decline

## 5 Speaking Role play

**Class activity** Role-play the situation. Then change roles.

**Group A:** You are salespeople. Offer help to the customers. Answer questions about prices.

**Group B:** You are customers. Decline help three times. Then accept help three times, and ask for the prices of three items.

 \$168.95

 \$23.99

 \$877.50

 \$40.89

 \$219.00

 \$9.25

A: *Can I help you?*
B: *No, thanks. I'm just looking.*
OR
A: *Can I help you?*
B: *Yes, please. How much . . . ?*

I can *accept and decline help.*

49

# C *What do you do for fun?*

## 1 **Vocabulary** Leisure activities and places

**A** 🔊 Listen and repeat.

eat out

go dancing

go shopping

hang out

play soccer

watch movies

**B** 🔊 Listen and repeat.

at a club

at a restaurant

at home

at the mall

in / at the park

**C Pair work** Do you do the activities in Part A? Where? Tell your partner.

**A:** *I watch movies at home. Do you?*
**B:** *Yes, I do. I watch movies at the mall, too.*

## 2 **Conversation** In our free time

🔊 Listen and practice.

**Annie:** What do you do for fun, Chad?
**Chad:** Oh, I hang out with friends.
**Annie:** Yeah? Where do you hang out?
**Chad:** At the mall. We sometimes watch a movie or go shopping. What about you?
**Annie:** I play soccer in the park.
**Chad:** Sounds fun. Who do you play with?
**Annie:** My brother and his friends. Actually, we need another player. Are you interested?
**Chad:** Yeah!

# 3 Grammar 🔊 Simple present *Wh-* questions with *do*

| | |
|---|---|
| **What do** you do for fun? <br> I hang out. | **Who do** you play soccer with? <br> My brother and his friends. |
| **Where do** you hang out? <br> At the mall. | **When do** you usually play soccer? <br> We usually play on weekends. |
| **How do** you get there? <br> We take the bus. | **Why do** you play soccer? <br> Because it's my favorite sport. |

**A** Read the answers. Write *Wh-* questions. Then practice with a partner.

1. *How do you get to class?*       I <u>take the bus</u> to class.
2. _____ I <u>eat out</u> on Friday night.
3. _____ I play sports with <u>my brother</u>.
4. _____ I go shopping <u>at the mall</u>.
5. _____ My friends and I watch movies <u>on Saturday</u>.
6. _____ I sometimes study with <u>my friends</u>.

**B Pair work** Ask and answer the questions in Part A. Answer with your own information.

A: *How do you get to class?*
B: *I usually walk, but I sometimes take the subway.*

# 4 Speaking Tell me more!

**A Pair work** Interview your partner. Take notes.

| Questions | Name: _____ |
|---|---|
| 1. When do you usually check your email? | |
| 2. What time do you go to bed on Sundays? | |
| 3. When do you chat with friends? | |
| 4. Who do you eat out with? Where do you go? | |
| 5. Where do you go shopping? How do you get there? | |
| 6. What do you do for fun on weekends? Why? | |

**B Pair work** Tell another classmate about your partner's answers. Are any of your partners' answers the same?

A: *Celia usually checks her email at night.*
B: *Luis checks his email at night, too.*

# 5 Keep talking!

Go to page 136 for more practice.

> *I can ask and answer questions about leisure activities.* ☑

# D Online fun

## 1 Reading ◄))

**A** Look at the pictures in the article. What do you see?

**B** Read the article. What's the best title? Check (✓) the correct answer.

☐ New Websites ☐ Chat Online ☐ Fun Online Activities

## Try one of these activities in your free time.

**BUY** 19.99

**1** *Buy and Sell*

What do you want? A new video game? A new phone? What *don't* you want? Your old jeans? Your old schoolbooks? Buy and sell things online!

**2**

Where is your best friend from elementary school now? Does your friend live in your city? Search his or her name, and find your friend.

**3**

Do you have pictures or movies on your cell phone or camera? Post them! Upload your favorite photos and videos for friends.

**4**

Tour a museum from your home! Go to the Egyptian Museum in Cairo, Barcelona's Picasso Museum, or Kyoto's National Museum.

**5**

Where do you want to go? Search the address and city, and find a map. Get directions to stores, parks, or a new restaurant.

**6**

Do you want a new album, your favorite song, or a new ringtone for your cell phone? Download it.

**C** Read the article again. Where do the headings go? Write them in the article.

| | | |
|---|---|---|
| Map it! | Take a Tour | Share Photos and Videos |
| Get Music | ✓ Buy and Sell | Find an Old Friend |

**D Pair work** What activities do you do online? Tell your partner.

*"I hardly ever sell things online, but I sometimes buy clothes online."*

## 2 Listening Four websites

**A** 🔊 Listen to Allison and James talk about the pictures on four websites.
Number the pictures from 1 to 4.

**B** 🔊 Listen again. Correct the false sentences.

　　　　　　　　　　*photos*
1. Allison looks at ~~videos~~ of Lorena Ochoa.
2. The Museum of Modern Art is in Paris.
3. James buys clothes on the website.
4. James often uploads videos.

## 3 Writing Let's chat!

**A** Choose a topic for a "chat": free time, online activities, or school. Create a user name. Then write a question about your topic.

**B Group work** Pass your question to the classmate on your right. Read and answer your classmate's question. Continue to pass, read, and answer all of the questions in your group.

> techgirl:  What do you do in your
>　　　　　　free time?
> jae-min:  I watch TV and play video games. My
>　　　　　　favorite video game is Soccer Star.
> jramirez:  I hardly ever play video games.
>　　　　　　I usually watch TV at night.
>　　　　　　My favorite show is . . .

**C Class activity** Tell the class about your chat.

## 4 Speaking My favorite website

**A Group work** Add a question about online habits to the list. Then ask and answer the questions.

- What's your favorite website?
- What other websites do you usually go to?
- Where do you upload your photos and videos?
- What news websites do you read?
- What blogs do you read?
- _____

**B Class activity** Share your information. Which websites are popular?

> *I can discuss how I use technology.* ✓

# Wrap-up

## 1 Quick pair review

**Lesson A Brainstorm!** Make a list of online activities. How many do you know? You have one minute.

**Lesson B Test your partner!** Write three prices and say them to your partner. Can your partner write them correctly? Check his or her answers. You have two minutes.

| My prices | My partner's prices |
|---|---|
| _____ | _____ |
| _____ | _____ |
| _____ | _____ |

**Lesson C Find out!** What are three activities both you and your partner do for fun? You have two minutes.

**A:** *I play soccer for fun. Do you?*
**B:** *No, I don't play soccer. Do you go shopping for fun?*
**A:** *Yes, sometimes.*

**Lesson D Do you remember?** Complete the sentences with the correct words. You have one minute.

| ✓Buy   Find   Share   Take |
|---|

1. _____*Buy*_____ and sell online.
2. _____ photos and videos.
3. _____ an old friend.
4. _____ a tour.

## 2 In the real world

How much are they? Find two different prices for each of these items. Then write about them.

| a belt | jeans | a small camera |
|---|---|---|
| a downloaded song | a laptop | an umbrella |

*Different Prices*
*A black belt is $29.99 at Style Shop.*
*It's $20.00 at Kelly's Accessories.*
*A downloaded song is . . .*

# Work and play

## Warm-up

**A** Where do the people usually work? Match the people and the places.

**B** Do you know any of the jobs in the pictures? Do you know any other jobs?

## 1 **Vocabulary** Jobs

**A** 🔊 Match the jobs and the people. Then listen and check your answers.

| | | | | | |
|---|---|---|---|---|---|
| a. accountant | c. doctor | e. flight attendant | g. pilot | i. receptionist | ✓k. waiter |
| b. cook / chef | d. electrician | f. nurse | h. police officer | j. taxi driver | l. waitress |

**B Pair work** Point to people in the pictures, and ask what their jobs are. Your partner says the jobs. Take turns.

**A:** *What's his job?*
**B:** *He's a waiter.*

## 2 **Language in context** At work

**A** 🔊 Read two job profiles. What are their jobs?

Lucia Ortega works in a hospital
from 11:00 p.m. to 7:00 a.m.
What does Lucia do? She's a nurse.

Henry Jenkins works in an office. He's an
accountant. What company does Henry work for?
He works for A1 Accountants.

**B** What about you? Do you have a job? What is it?

56

# 3 Grammar 🔊 | Simple present *Wh-* questions with *does*

| | |
|---|---|
| **What does** Lucia **do**? <br> She's a nurse. | **Where does** Henry **work**? <br> He works in an office. |
| **When does** she **work**? <br> She works from 11:00 to 7:00. | **What** company **does** Henry **work** for? <br> He works for A1 Accountants. |

**A** Complete the conversations with the correct words. Then practice with a partner.

1. **A:** ___What___ does your brother ___do___ ?

   **B:** Oh, Tom's a doctor.

   **A:** Really? _____ does he _____ ?

   **B:** He works in a hospital.

2. **A:** _____ does Sue _____ ?

   **B:** On Mondays, Wednesdays, and Fridays.

   **A:** And _____ company does she _____ for?

   **B:** She works for Town Bank.

**B Pair work** Write questions about Mr. Miller, Lisa, and Nicole. Then ask and answer them.

 Mr. Miller

 Lisa

 STAR COMPUTERS · Nicole

| | | |
|---|---|---|
| What ___does Mr. Miller do___ ? | What _____ ? | Where _____ ? |
| Where _____ ? | When _____ ? | What company _____ ? |

**A:** *What does Mr. Miller do?*
**B:** *He's an English teacher.*

# 4 Speaking People's jobs

**Class activity** Add two jobs to the chart. Then find classmates who know people with those jobs. Ask for more information.

| Job | Classmate | Person | Extra information |
|---|---|---|---|
| chef | | | |
| nurse | | | |
| police officer | | | |
| taxi driver | | | |
| | | | |
| | | | |

**A:** *Do you know a chef?*
**B:** *Yes. My friend Marco is a chef.*

**A:** *Where does he work?*
**B:** *He works at Speedy Sushi.*

# 5 Keep talking!

Go to page **137** for more practice.

Go to page **137** for more practice.

*I can identify and talk about jobs.* ✓

# B Can I speak to . . . ?

## 1 Interactions — On the phone

**A** Look at the pictures. Where does Ed work?

**B** 🔊 Listen and practice.

**Ed:** Good morning, Ace Accountants.
**Ashley:** Hello. Can I speak to Laura Reed?
**Ed:** Who is this, please?
**Ashley:** It's Ashley Tillman.

**Ed:** Just a minute, please. . . . Oh, I'm sorry. Ms. Reed is in a meeting.
**Ashley:** All right. Thank you.

**C** 🔊 Listen to the expressions. Then practice the conversation again with the new expressions.

### Asking for someone on the phone

Can I speak to . . . ?
Could I please speak to . . . ?
Is . . . there?

### Having someone wait

Just a minute, please.
Hold on, please.
One moment, please.

**D Pair work** Practice the conversation again with the names below.

Gabriela Garcia

Anthony Davis

Kumiko Takahashi

Roberto Santos

**A:** *Good morning, Ace Accountants.*
**B:** *Hello. Can I speak to Gabriela Garcia?*
**A:** *Who is this, please?*

## 2 **Listening** A busy woman

**A** 🔊 Listen to Kevin call Star Computers on five different days. Where is Ellen Astor each day? Number the pictures from 1 to 5.

at lunch

1

in a meeting

on another line

on vacation

with a customer

**B** 🔊 Listen again. How does Kevin ask to speak to Ellen Astor? Number the questions from 1 to 5.

_____ Is Ms. Astor there?                  _____ Can I speak to Ellen Astor?

_____ Could I please speak to . . . ?        _____ Could I speak to Ms. Astor, please?

_1_ Can I please speak to Ellen Astor?

## 3 **Speaking** Role play

**Pair work** Role-play the situation. Then change roles.

**Student A:** You are a receptionist at Sun Travel. Answer the phone. Tell the caller to wait, and then say why the person can't talk.

**Student B:** Call Sun Travel. Imagine someone you know works there. Ask to speak to the person.

**A:** *Hello, Sun Travel.*
**B:** *Hi. Can I please speak to Jackie Miller?*
**A:** *Of course. Just a minute, please. . . .*
   *I'm sorry. Jackie's with a customer.*
**B:** *Oh, OK. Thanks.*

> I can **ask for someone on the telephone.** ☑
>
> I can **have someone wait.** ☑

## C Can you sing?

### 1 Vocabulary Abilities

**A** 🔊 Listen and repeat.

dance

draw

fix computers

paint

play the guitar

sing

speak French

*Où est la piscine?*

swim

**B Pair work** What things do you sometimes do? Tell your partner.

### 2 Conversation Top talent?

🔊 Listen and practice.

**Host:** Welcome to *Top Talent*. What's your name, please?

**Pamela:** Hello. My name is Pamela Wells.

**Host:** Tell us, can you sing, Pamela?

**Pamela:** No, I can't sing at all.

**Host:** Well, can you play an instrument? the guitar? the piano?

**Pamela:** No, I can't.

**Host:** You can't sing, and you can't play an instrument. What *can* you do, Pamela?

**Pamela:** I can dance!

**Host:** Great! Let's see.

## 3 Grammar 🔊 *Can* for ability; *and, but,* and *or*

| I | | | **Can** you sing? |
|---|---|---|---|
| You | | | Yes, I **can**.     No, I **can't**. |
| He | **can** | dance very well. | What **can** Pamela do? |
| She | **can't** | sing at all. | She **can** dance, **and** she **can** swim. |
| We | | | She **can** dance, **but** she **can't** sing. |
| They | | | She **can't** sing **or** play an instrument. |

**A** Read the answers. Write the questions. Then practice with a partner.

1. *Can Jenny swim?* _____   No, Jenny can't swim.
2. _____   Billy can fix computers.
3. _____   Yes, Tom and Jill can sing very well.
4. _____   No, I can't play an instrument.
5. _____   Jay and I can dance and speak French.
6. _____   No, Sally can't paint at all.

**B Pair work** Make six sentences about Frank with *and, but,* or *or.* Tell your partner.

Frank's Abilities

✓ draw      X sing      ✓ swim
X paint     X dance     ✓ play the guitar        *"Frank can draw, but . . ."*

## 4 Pronunciation *Can* and *can't*

**A** 🔊 Listen and repeat. Notice the pronunciation of *can* /kən/ and *can't* /kænt/.

I can draw.     I can't paint.     I can draw, but I can't paint.

**B** 🔊 Listen to the conversations. Do you hear *can* or *can't*? Circle the correct answers.

1. can / (can't)     2. can / can't     3. can / can't     4. can / can't

## 5 Speaking Can you paint?

**A Pair work** Add two abilities to the chart. Then interview your partner. Check (✓) the things he or she can do.

| Can you . . . ? | | | |
|---|---|---|---|
| ☐ paint | ☐ upload a video | ☐ sing in English | ☐ ride a bicycle |
| ☐ draw | ☐ dance | ☐ play an instrument | ☐ |
| ☐ swim | ☐ drive | ☐ fix a car | ☐ |

**B Pair work** Tell another classmate about your partner's abilities. Can your partner do something that you can't? What is it?

## 6 Keep talking!

Go to page 138 for more practice.

*I can* describe my talents and abilities. ☑

## D Work and study

### 1 Reading 🔊

**A** Look at the pictures. Where do they work? Guess.

**B** Read the article. Where are Jin-hee, Ramiro, and Aisha now?

# OVERSEAS OPPORTUNITIES
## FOR STUDENTS

### Be an Intern

You work for a short time in a company or an organization. You sometimes get a small salary as an intern.

Jin-hee is from South Korea and has an internship with a publishing company in New York City. The company makes French books. Jin-hee answers the phone and makes photocopies.

### Study and Work

In this program, you can study *and* work. You usually study in the morning and work in the afternoon or evening.

Ramiro is from Mexico. He's in Australia now. He studies computer science part-time and works part-time. He takes classes in the morning and fixes computers in the evening. He works 20 hours a week.

### Volunteer

Some organizations need extra help. Volunteers usually don't get a salary for their work.

Aisha is from Egypt. She's on a volunteer program in Nigeria at a school for children. She teaches classes, and she helps the children with their schoolwork. She works full-time from Monday to Friday.

**C** Read the article again. Answer the questions.

1. Do people get a salary as an intern? *They sometimes get a small salary.*
2. What does Jin-hee do as an intern? _____
3. In study and work programs, when do people usually work? _____
4. What does Ramiro study? _____
5. Do volunteers usually get a salary for their work? _____
6. What does Aisha do as a volunteer? _____

**D Pair work** Do people come to your country from other countries to study or work? What do they do? Discuss your ideas.

## 2 Listening Exciting opportunities

**A** 🔊 Listen to two students discuss three advertisements. Number them from 1 to 3.

**Volunteer!**

Are you interested in animals? Can you swim? _____ with turtles in Costa Rica. Work _____ to Saturday, 6:00 a.m. to _____ p.m. For more information, send an email to **CRVolunteer@cup.edu**

**Be an Intern**

Are you 18 to _____ years old? Can you speak Chinese, _____ , Japanese, or English? Be an intern at a theme _____ in Hong Kong!

Email us at **hongkong@cup.com/intern**

**Study and Work**

Can you cook? Come to Rome. Study Italian in the morning, and work in a restaurant in the _evening_ . See the city in your _____ time! _____ salary.

Contact us at **study&work@cambridge.org** [1]

**B** 🔊 Listen again. Complete the sentences with the correct words.

## 3 Writing My abilities

**A** Make lists of things you can and can't do well. Then write a paragraph about your abilities. Use the model and your lists to help you.

> *My Abilities*
> *I can play sports. I can play basketball and tennis very well. My favorite sport is soccer, but I can't play it very well. I can't play golf at all!*

**B Pair work** Share your paragraphs. Ask and answer questions for more information.

## 4 Speaking How well can you . . . ?

**Group work** Discuss the overseas opportunities in Exercise 1, Exercise 2, or your own ideas.

- What abilities do you need in each program?
- How well can you do each thing? (very well? well? not well? not at all?)
- Are any of the programs right for you?

*I can talk about study and work programs.* ✓

# Wrap-up

## 1 Quick pair review

**Lesson A** **Guess!** Describe a job, but don't say what it is. Can your partner guess it? Take turns. You have two minutes.

**A:** *This person drives a car.*
**B:** *Is he a police officer?*
**A:** *No. The car is yellow in New York City.*
**B:** *Is he a taxi driver?*
**A:** *Yes.*

**Lesson B** **Brainstorm!** Make a list of ways to ask for someone on the phone and have someone wait. You have two minutes.

**Lesson C** **Find out!** What are two things both you and your partner can do? What are two things you can't do? You have two minutes.

**A:** *Can you cook?*
**B:** *Not really. Can you?*
**A:** *No, I can't!*

**Lesson D** **Do you remember?** Are the sentences true or false? Write T (true) or F (false). You have two minutes.

1. Volunteers usually get a salary. __F__

2. Volunteers always work part-time. _____

3. Interns work for companies or organizations. _____

4. Interns never get a salary. _____

## 2 In the real world

Go online and find information in English about an overseas program. Then write about it.

- What is the name of the program?
- Where is the program?
- What kind of program is it?
- What do people do in the program?

> *The Peace Corps*
> *The Peace Corps is an overseas program.*
> *Americans volunteer in many countries.*
> *They help build things and teach people.*

# Food

## Warm-up

**A** Match the words and the pictures.

1. Italian food __c__    2. Mexican food _____    3. Chinese food _____    4. Japanese food _____

**B** Name ten food words you know.

## 1 **Vocabulary** Food

**A** 🔊 Match the words and the pictures. Then listen and check your answers.

| | | | |
|---|---|---|---|
| a. apples | e. carrots | i. eggs | m. pasta |
| b. bananas | f. cereal | j. fish | n. potatoes |
| c. beans | ✓g. cheese | k. milk | o. rice |
| d. beef | h. chicken | l. noodles | p. tomatoes |

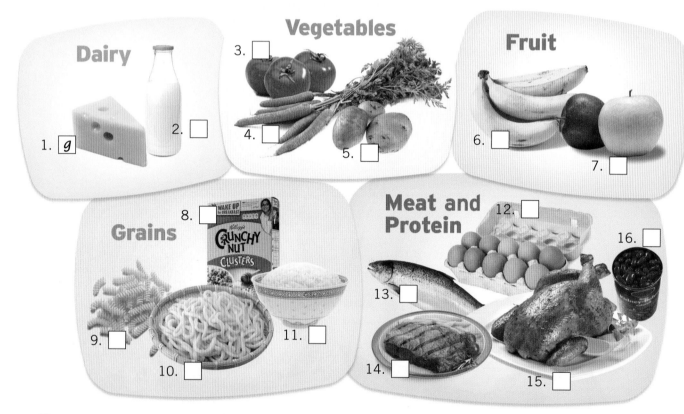

Dairy
1. g  2. ☐

Vegetables
3. ☐  4. ☐  5. ☐

Fruit
6. ☐  7. ☐

Grains
8. ☐  9. ☐  10. ☐  11. ☐

Meat and Protein
12. ☐  13. ☐  14. ☐  15. ☐  16. ☐

**B** **Pair work** Do you ever eat the food in Part A? Tell your partner.

*"I often eat apples. I sometimes eat eggs. I never eat noodles."*

## 2 **Language in context** Favorite meals

**A** 🔊 Listen to three people talk about their favorite meals. Underline the food words.

I love breakfast. I usually eat some cereal, but I don't have any milk with it. I also eat an apple.

My favorite meal is lunch. I don't have a lot of time, so I often just get some noodles.

My favorite meal of the day is dinner. A typical dinner for me is rice and beans with some beef.

**B** What about you? What's your favorite meal of the day? What do you eat?

# 3 Grammar  **Count and noncount nouns; *some* and *any***

| Count nouns | Noncount nouns |
|---|---|

**Count nouns**

an apple    a tomato

apples   tomatoes

Do you have **any** apples?
  Yes, I have **some** (apples).
  No, I don't have **any** (apples).

**Noncount nouns**

milk   cereal

Do you have **any** milk?
  Yes, I have **some** (milk).
  No, I don't have **any** (milk).

**A** Complete the chart with the food words from Exercise 1. Then compare with a partner.

**Count nouns**

_____apples_____   _____
_____tomatoes_____   _____
_____   _____
_____   _____

**Noncount nouns**

_____milk_____   _____
_____cereal_____   _____
_____   _____
_____   _____

**B** Circle the correct words. Then practice with a partner.

A: What do you want for lunch, Amy?
B: Let's just make **some** / **any** pasta.
A: Good idea. We have **some** / **any** pasta.
B: Let's see. We have **some** / **any** carrots. We don't have **some** / **any** tomatoes.
A: OK, I can get **some** / **any** at the store. What else?
B: Do we have **some** / **any** cheese?
A: No, we don't have **some** / **any**. I can get **some** / **any**.

**C Pair work** Practice the conversation again. Use other food words from Exercise 1.

# 4 Speaking What do you eat?

**A** Write your answers to the questions in the chart.

| What do you often eat for . . . ? | Me | Name: _____ | Name: _____ |
|---|---|---|---|
| breakfast | | | |
| lunch | | | |
| dinner | | | |

**B Group work** Interview two classmates. Complete the chart with their answers.

# 5 Keep talking!

Go to page 139 for more practice.

I can say what meals I eat.

# B I like Chinese food!

## 1 Interactions — Likes and dislikes

**A** Look at the pictures. Where are Maria and Tom?

**B** 🔊 Listen and practice.

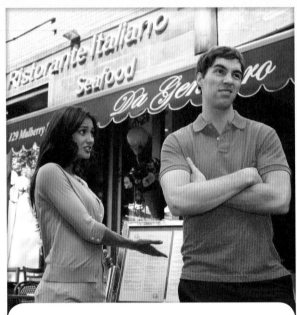

**Maria:** Do you like pasta?
**Tom:** No, I don't like Italian food.

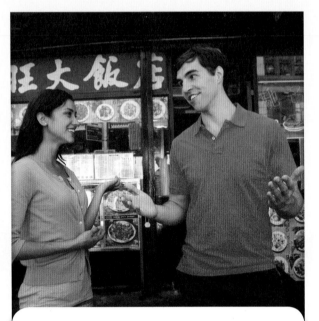

**Maria:** How about Chinese food?
**Tom:** Good idea. I like Chinese food!

**C** 🔊 Listen to the expressions. Then practice the conversation again with the new expressions.

### Expressing dislikes

🙁 I don't like . . .

🙁 I don't like . . . at all.

😠 I hate . . . !

### Expressing likes

🙂 I like . . .

😊 I really like . . .

😍 I love . . . !

**D Pair work** Look at Maria's and Tom's likes and dislikes. Are they the same as yours? Tell your partner.

| | 😍 | 😊 | 🙂 | 🙁 | 🙁 | 😠 |
|---|---|---|---|---|---|---|
| **Maria** | fish | Mexican food | Japanese food | milk | beans | beef |
| **Tom** | cheese | carrots | Chinese food | Italian food | French food | eggs |

*"Maria loves fish, but I don't like fish at all."*

68

## 2 Pronunciation Word stress

**A** 🔊 Listen and repeat. Notice the stress in the words.

| ● | ●● | ●●● |
|---|---|---|
| **cheese** | **a**pple | ba**na**na |
| **beans** | **chi**cken | po**ta**to |
| **beef** | **noo**dles | to**ma**to |
| _____ | _____ | _____ |
| _____ | _____ | |

**B** 🔊 Listen. Complete the chart with the correct words.

dairy      fruit      Italian      meat      pasta

## 3 Listening I love it!

**A** 🔊 Listen to four conversations about food. Check (✓) the words you hear.

1. ☐ beans     2. ☐ cheese     3. ☐ noodles     4. ☐ bananas
   ✓ beef         ☐ chicken       ☐ potatoes      ☐ carrots
   ✓ pasta       ☐ eggs          ☐ tomatoes     ☐ cereal

**B** 🔊 Listen again. Do the two speakers like the same things?
Circle the correct answers.

1. yes / (no)     2. yes / no     3. yes / no     4. yes / no

## 4 Speaking What do you like?

**A** Make a list of food you like and food you don't like.

| Food I like | Food I don't like |
|---|---|
| 🙂 | 🙁 |
| 😊 | 😕 |
| 😍 | 😣 |

**B Pair work** Tell your partner about the food you like and don't like.
Ask and answer questions for more information.

   A: *I really like fish.*
   B: *Do you cook fish at home?*
   A: *No, I don't. I eat fish in restaurants.*

*I can say what I like and dislike.* ☑

# C Meals

## 1 Vocabulary More food

**A** 🔊 Label the pictures with the correct words. Then listen and check your answers.

| dumplings | ✓hot dogs | pizza | soup | sushi |
|---|---|---|---|---|
| hamburgers | pancakes | salad | spaghetti | tacos |

1. _hot dogs_   2. _____   3. _____   4. _____   5. _____

6. _____   7. _____   8. _____   9. _____   10. _____

**B Pair work** Which food in Part A do you like? Which food don't you like? Compare your answers.

**A:** *I really like dumplings. Do you?*
**B:** *Yes, I like dumplings, too. Do you like . . . ?*

## 2 Conversation I eat pizza every day.

🔊 Listen and practice.

**Megan:** What is that?
**David:** Pizza. My father is a pizza chef.
**Megan:** Really? So how often do you eat pizza?
**David:** I eat pizza every day. It's my favorite food!
**Megan:** I don't eat pizza very often, but it looks interesting. What's on it?
**David:** Cheese, tomatoes, black beans, and fish.
**Megan:** Black beans and fish on pizza. Yuck!
**David:** Have some. It's really good.
**Megan:** No, thanks. I'm not very hungry.

# 3 Grammar 🔊 *How often*; time expressions

**How often** do you eat pizza?

| | |
|---|---|
| I eat pizza | **every day**. **once a week**. **twice a month**. **three times a month**. **once in a while**. |
| I do**n't** eat pizza **very often**. I **never** eat pizza. | |

**A** Look at Matt's menu. Answer the questions. Then practice with a partner.

Matt's Menu

| | Monday | Tuesday | Wednesday | Thursday | Friday | Saturday | Sunday |
|---|---|---|---|---|---|---|---|
| Breakfast | cereal | eggs | cereal | eggs | cereal | pancakes | pancakes |
| Lunch | soup | pizza | soup | sushi | soup | tacos | sushi |
| Dinner | dumplings | chicken | beef | chicken | pizza | spaghetti | hamburgers |

1. How often does Matt eat hamburgers for dinner?   *He eats hamburgers once a week.*
2. How often does Matt eat soup for lunch?   _____
3. How often does Matt eat pancakes?   _____
4. How often does Matt eat hot dogs?   _____
5. How often does Matt eat sushi for lunch?   _____
6. How often does Matt eat dumplings for dinner?   _____

**B Pair work** Make six sentences about your eating habits with different time expressions. Tell your partner.

*"I eat spaghetti once a month."*

# 4 Speaking Eating habits

**A** Add three food words to the chart. Then answer the questions.

| How often do you eat . . . ? | Me | | Name: _____ | |
|---|---|---|---|---|
| hot dogs | | | | |
| salad | | | | |
| tacos | | | | |
| | | | | |
| | | | | |
| | | | | |

**B Pair work** Interview your partner. Complete the chart with his or her answers.

**C Pair work** Compare your information with another partner.

*"Kazu eats hot dogs once a week, but I eat them once in a while."*

# 5 Keep talking!

Go to page 140 for more practice.

I can talk about my eating habits. ☑

# D Favorite food

## 1 Reading

**A** Look at the pictures in the magazine article. Can you name the food?

**B** Read the article. What's the best title? Check (✓) the correct answer.

☐ Meal Times    ☐ My Favorite Food    ☐ Dinner Around the World

### Letters from our readers

I love nachos. I make them once a week. I just buy some tortilla chips and put cheese, beef, tomatoes, and onions on top. Then I cook it in the microwave.

**HEATHER**
*United States*

I like dumplings a lot. You can buy good dumplings in restaurants, but I usually eat my mother's dumplings. They're delicious! I eat them for lunch four or five times a month.

**JAE-SUN**
*South Korea*

My wife and I go to our favorite ice-cream shop three times a month. They have many flavors, but we always get chocolate ice cream. It's our favorite.

**CARLOS**
*Argentina*

I really like pancakes, but we don't eat them for breakfast. We eat them after dinner. We usually eat them two or three times a month. I like to eat them with jam.

**OLGA**
*Sweden*

**C** Read the article again. Complete the chart with the correct information.

|  | Favorite food | How often they have it |
|---|---|---|
| Heather | *nachos* | *once a week* |
| Jae-sun | | |
| Carlos | | |
| Olga | | |

**D Pair work** Imagine you can have one food in Part A right now. Which food do you want? Why? Tell your partner.

*"I want dumplings. I love Korean food. Vegetable dumplings are my favorite."*

## 2 Listening A meal in Sweden

**A** 🔊 Listen to Olga describe a typical meal in Sweden.
Which meal does she talk about? Check (✓) the correct answer.

☐ breakfast    ☐ lunch    ☐ dinner

**B** 🔊 Listen again. Circle the words you hear.

| | | | | | |
|---|---|---|---|---|---|
| beans | (bread) | cheese | fish | milk | pancakes |
| beef | cereal | eggs | fruit | noodles | potatoes |

## 3 Writing A typical meal

**A** Think of a typical meal in your country. Answer the questions.

- What do people drink? _____
- What do people eat? _____
- Do *you* usually eat it? _____
- Why or why not? _____

**B** Write about a typical meal in your country.
Use the model and your answers in Part A to help you.

**C Class activity** Post your writing around the room.
Read your classmates' writing. Who describes similar meals?

*A Japanese Breakfast*
*People in Japan usually drink green tea for breakfast. They eat fish, rice, soup, salad, and pickles. It's a healthy and delicious breakfast, but I don't eat this. I usually drink orange juice and eat cereal and fruit for breakfast.*

## 4 Speaking What's your favorite meal?

**A Pair work** Add two questions about food to the chart. Then interview your partner. Take notes.

| Questions | Name: _____ |
|---|---|
| What's your favorite meal? | |
| What's your favorite kind of food? | |
| How often do you have it? | |
| Who makes it? | |
| Can you cook it? | |
| What do you drink with it? | |
| | |
| | |

A: *What's your favorite kind of food?*
B: *I love Mexican food.*

**B Group work** Tell your group about your partner's favorite meal.
Do you like that meal, too? Does your group like it?

*I can talk about my favorite food.* ☑

# Wrap-up

## 1 Quick pair review

**Lesson A** **Brainstorm!** Make a list of count and noncount food words. How many do you know? You have one minute.

**Lesson B** **Do you remember?** Look at the pictures. Complete the sentences with the correct words. You have one minute.

I _don't like_ fish _at all_ .         I _____ French food.

I _____ _____ beef.         I _____ _____ breakfast.

I _____ milk!         I _____ carrots!

**Lesson C** **Find out!** What is one thing both you and your partner eat every week? eat once in a while? never eat? You have two minutes.

A: *I eat rice every week. Do you?*
B: *Yes, I do.*

**Lesson D** **Guess!** Describe your favorite food, but don't say its name! Can your partner guess what it is? Take turns. You have two minutes.

A: *I love this food. It's Italian, and I eat it once in a while. I eat it at home.*
B: *Is it pasta?*
A: *Yes.*

## 2 In the real world

Go online and find information in English about your favorite movie star's or musician's eating habits. Then write about them.

- What is his or her favorite food?
- How often does he or she usually eat it?

*Jack Black's Favorite Food*
*The American actor Jack Black doesn't have*
*one favorite food. He has two of them! He*
*loves pizza and cheeseburgers.*

# In the neighborhood

## Warm-up

**A** Look at the picture. Make six sentences about it.

**B** Where can you do these things?

| buy glasses | buy some fruit | check email | eat lunch | get a book | see a movie |

# A Around town

## 1 Vocabulary Places in the neighborhood

**A** ◀))) Match the words and the places. Then listen and check your answers.

| | | | |
|---|---|---|---|
| a. bank | c. bus stop | e. gas station ✓g. library | i. subway station |
| b. bookstore | d. coffee shop | f. hotel  h. newsstand | j. supermarket |

**B Pair work** Which places are in your school's neighborhood?

*"We have a coffee shop, some restaurants, and a . . ."*

## 2 Language in context Ads

**A** ◀))) Read three advertisements for places in a neighborhood. What places do they describe?

**Mama's Place**

Come to Mama's Place
for real Italian food.

On Second Avenue
**10% off**
between 5:30 and 6:30 p.m.

**ABC Supermarket**
*WE'RE ALWAYS OPEN!*

**Find everything you need
at ABC Supermarket!**

New location next to
Town Bank

**JOE'S COFFEE SHOP**

**Best coffee in town!**
Find us on the corner of
Main St. and First Ave.

**B** What can you do at each place in Part A?

# 3 Grammar 🔊 Prepositions of location

| in | on | next to | across from | between | on the corner of |

The newsstand is **in** the park.
The gas station is **on** Second Avenue.
The supermarket is **next to** the bank.
The bus stop is **across from** the park.

The hotel is **between** the restaurant and the bookstore.
The coffee shop is **on the corner of** Main Street and First Avenue.

Look at the map in Exercise 1. Complete the sentences with the correct prepositions.

1. The newsstand is _____*in*_____ the park.
2. The subway station is _____ the park.
3. The bookstore is _____ the hotel.
4. Mama's Place is _____ Second Avenue.
5. The gas station is _____ Second Avenue and Grand Street.
6. The library is _____ the coffee shop and the bus stop.

# 4 Pronunciation Word stress

🔊 Listen and repeat. Notice the stress on the first or last syllable.

| ●● | | ●● |
|---|---|---|
| **book**store | **news**stand | a**cross** |
| **co**ffee | **sta**tion | be**tween** |
| **cor**ner | **sub**way | ho**tel** |

# 5 Speaking Where's the drugstore?

**A Pair work** Add these four places to the map in Exercise 1. Then ask and answer questions about their locations.

| drugstore | post office | Internet café | department store |

A: *Where's the drugstore on your map?*
B: *It's next to the bank. Where is it on your map?*

**B Pair work** Where are the places in your town? Tell your partner.

# 6 Keep talking!

Student A go to page 141 and Student B go to page 142 for more practice.

*I can* give the locations of neighborhood places. ☑

# B  *How do I get to . . . ?*

## 1 Giving directions

**A** 🔊 Listen and repeat.

1
**Go up** Main Street.
**Turn left** on Ninth Street.
**Go** one block.
It's **on the right**, next to a school.

2
**Walk down** Main Street.
**Take a right** on Fifth Street.
**Walk** two blocks.
It's **on the left**, across from the park.

**B Pair work** Give directions from *Start* to the coffee shop and the bus station.

## 2 Interactions  Directions

**A** 🔊 Listen and practice.

**Alex:** Excuse me. How do I get to the park?
**Laura:** Go down Seventh Street and take a left on Elm Street. Walk one block to Sixth Street. It's on the right, across from the bus station.
**Alex:** Turn left on Elm Street?
**Laura:** Yes.
**Alex:** Great! Thank you very much.

**B** 🔊 Listen to the expressions. Then practice the conversation again with the new expression.

### Asking for directions

How do I get to . . . ?
How can I get to . . . ?

# 3 Listening Follow the route

**A** 🔊 Listen to Carl and Alice use their GPS to get from Pioneer Square to the library in Seattle. Follow their route. Then mark an ✗ at the library.

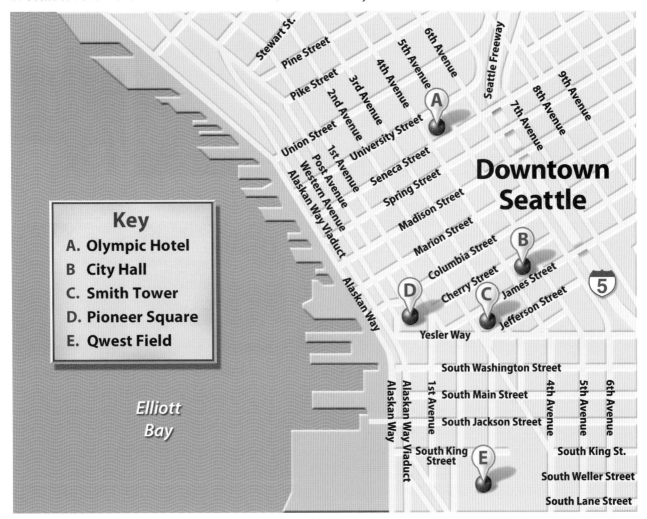

**Key**

A. Olympic Hotel
B City Hall
C. Smith Tower
D. Pioneer Square
E. Qwest Field

**B** 🔊 Listen to Carl and Alice go from the library to Pike Place Market. Follow their route. Then mark a ✓ at the market.

**C Pair work** Give directions from Pioneer Square to other places on the map. Your partner follows them. Take turns.

# 4 Speaking How do I get to . . . ?

**A Pair work** Draw a simple map of the neighborhood around your school. Label different places and street names.

**B Pair work** Role-play the situation. Then change roles.

Student A: You are a tourist in town. Ask for directions to places in the neighborhood.
Student B: You meet a tourist in your town. Give him or her directions to places in your neighborhood. Start at your school.

A: *How do I get to the train station?*
B: *Walk down Main Street . . .*

I can *ask for and give directions.*

# C Fun in the city

## 1 Vocabulary Places to visit

**A** ◀))) Listen and repeat.

amusement park

aquarium

movie theater

museum

science center

swimming pool

water park

zoo

**B Pair work** How often do you go to each place? Tell your partner.

*"Our town has a swimming pool, but I hardly ever go there."*

## 2 Conversation Tourist information

◀))) Listen and practice.

**Larry:** Hello. Can I help you?

**Maggie:** Yes. Is there a museum near here?

**Larry:** Let's see. . . . Yes. There's a museum across from the park.

**Maggie:** And is there an aquarium in this city?

**Larry:** Yes, there is. It's near the museum. It's a very nice aquarium.

**Maggie:** Great. I have one more question. Are there any amusement parks?

**Larry:** There aren't any amusement parks, but there's a nice water park.

# 3 Grammar 🔊 *There is, there are*

| | |
|---|---|
| **There's** a museum. | **There are** two swimming pools. |
| **There isn't** an amusement park. | **There aren't** any good zoos in this city. |
| **Is there** an aquarium in this city? | **Are there** any swimming pools near here? |
| Yes, **there is**.　No, **there isn't**. | Yes, **there are**.　No, **there aren't**. |

*Contraction*  There's = There is

**A** Complete the questions about the city with *Is there a / an . . . ?* or
*Are there any . . . ?* Then compare with a partner.

1. _Is there a_ _____ zoo?
2. _____ water parks?
3. _____ aquarium?
4. _____ museums?
5. _____ amusement park?
6. _____ movie theaters?

**B Pair work** Ask and answer the questions in Part A.
Use the map on the right.

　　A: *Is there a zoo?*
　　B: *Yes, there is. There's one zoo.*

# 4 Speaking Is there . . . ? Are there . . . ?

**A Pair work** Add two items to the chart. Then interview your partner. Check (✓)
the places that are in his or her neighborhood, and ask for more information.

| | Places | Locations | Extra information |
|---|---|---|---|
| ☐ | movie theaters | | |
| ☐ | museums | | |
| ☐ | science center | | |
| ☐ | swimming pool | | |
| ☐ | | | |
| ☐ | | | |

　　A: *Are there any movie theaters in your neighborhood?*
　　B: *Yes, there's one. It's on University Avenue.*
　　A: *How often do you go there?*

**B Class activity** Tell the class about two interesting places in your
partner's neighborhood.

# 5 Keep talking!

Go to page 143 for more practice.

*I can* talk about interesting places in my town. ✓

# D A great place to visit

## 1 Reading

**A** Is there an aquarium in your town or city? If yes, do you like it? If no, do you want one?

**B** Read the poster. Where is the Monterey Bay Aquarium?

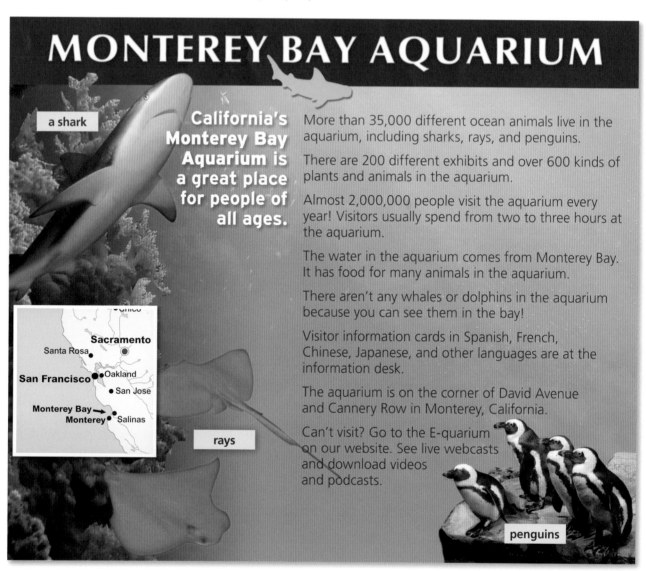

**MONTEREY BAY AQUARIUM**

a shark

**California's Monterey Bay Aquarium is a great place for people of all ages.**

More than 35,000 different ocean animals live in the aquarium, including sharks, rays, and penguins.

There are 200 different exhibits and over 600 kinds of plants and animals in the aquarium.

Almost 2,000,000 people visit the aquarium every year! Visitors usually spend from two to three hours at the aquarium.

The water in the aquarium comes from Monterey Bay. It has food for many animals in the aquarium.

There aren't any whales or dolphins in the aquarium because you can see them in the bay!

Visitor information cards in Spanish, French, Chinese, Japanese, and other languages are at the information desk.

The aquarium is on the corner of David Avenue and Cannery Row in Monterey, California.

Can't visit? Go to the E-quarium on our website. See live webcasts and download videos and podcasts.

Chico
Sacramento
Santa Rosa
San Francisco • Oakland
• San Jose
Monterey Bay →
Monterey • Salinas

rays

penguins

**C** Read the poster again. Answer the questions.

1. What animals live in the aquarium? _Sharks, rays, and penguins live in the aquarium._
2. Where does the aquarium's water come from? _____
3. Are there any whales or dolphins in the aquarium? _____
4. Where are the visitor information cards? _____
5. What is on their website? _____

**D Pair work** What is your favorite place to visit in your town or city? Why? Tell your partner.

*"I like the modern art museum because it has cool paintings. I go to the museum once a month."*

## 2 Listening City information

**A** 🔊 Listen to three tourists ask for information about two places in the city. Write the places in the chart.

|  | Place 1 | Place 2 |
|---|---|---|
| 1. | (movie theater) | |
| 2. | | |
| 3. | | |

**B** 🔊 Listen again. Which places are in the city? Circle the correct answers.

## 3 Writing and speaking Group poster presentation

**A Group work** Choose an interesting place in your city. What do you know about it? Make a list.

**B Group work** Create and design a poster about the place. Use your list from Part A.

## COME TO THE IMAGINE SCIENCE CENTER!
### Great for kids, teens, and adults.

- We're open every day from 9:00 to 6:00.
- There's a free audio tour in ten languages.
- There's an excellent café in the museum.
- Try our science experiments.
- Learn about plant life.
- There are over 10,000 books in the bookstore.

**C Class activity** Present your posters. Ask and answer questions for more information.

**A:** *The Imagine Science Center is a great place to visit.*
**B:** *It's open every day from 9:00 to 6:00.*
**C:** *There's a free audio tour. You can listen to the tour in ten languages.*
**D:** *Where is the Imagine Science Center?*
**C:** *It's at 367 First Avenue, near the park.*

> *I can* give a presentation on a city attraction. ☑

# Wrap-up

## 1 Quick pair review

**Lesson A Brainstorm!** Make a list of places in a neighborhood. How many do you know? You have one minute.

**Lesson B Do you remember?** Circle the correct answers. You have two minutes.

A: Excuse me. **Where / (How)** do I get to the library from here?
B: Walk up Third Avenue and **turn / take** left on Elm Street.
A: Is the library on Elm Street?
B: No, it's not. **Go / Turn** two blocks on Elm Street. Then **take / walk** a right on Main Street. The library is **on / in** the right.
A: Thanks!

**Lesson C Find out!** What are two kinds of places both you and your partner like to visit in your city or other cities? What are two kinds of places you don't like to visit? You have two minutes.

A: *I like museums. Do you?*
B: *Not really. How about water parks? I love those!*
A: *I do, too!*

**Lesson D Guess!** Describe a place to visit in your area, but don't say its name! Can your partner guess the name? Take turns. You have two minutes.

A: *I go there with my friends on weekends.*
B: *Is it Mall Marina?*
A: *No. There are rides and games there.*
B: *Is it the amusement park, Fantasy Land?*
A: *Yes!*

## 2 In the real world

What zoos do you know? Go online and find information in English about a zoo. Then write about it.

- What is the name of the zoo? Where is it?
- What animals and exhibits are there?
- Can you watch videos or take a tour on the website?

> *The San Diego Zoo*
> *The San Diego Zoo is a famous zoo in California. You can see pandas there. You can also . . .*

# What are you doing?

## Warm-up

**A** Look at the picture. Make eight sentences about it.

**B** Do you ever do these things on a subway, train, or bus?

# I'm looking for you.

## 1 Vocabulary Actions and prepositions

**A** 🔊 Listen and repeat.

start          hold          look for          wave

sit          stand          run          end

**B** 🔊 Listen and repeat.

behind          in          in front of          on          under

**C Pair work** Tell your partner to sit and stand in different places in the classroom.
Use the prepositions. Take turns.

*"Stand in front of the door."*

## 2 Language in context Meeting a friend

**A** 🔊 Listen to Amy and Claudio meet at a soccer game. Where is Amy? Where is Claudio?

**Amy:** Hi, Claudio. It's Amy. I'm standing under the scoreboard. Where are you?

**Claudio:** I'm sitting in front of the big clock. Do you see me?

**Amy:** No, I don't.

**Claudio:** Well, I'm wearing a red shirt.

**Amy:** But, Claudio, everyone is wearing a red shirt!

**B** What about you? Where do you usually meet your friends at big games or other events?

# 3 Grammar 🔊 Present continuous statements

| | | |
|---|---|---|
| I'm **standing** under the scoreboard. | I'm **not sitting**. | *Spelling* |
| You're **running**. | You're **not walking**. | run → run**ning** |
| He's **sitting** in front of the big clock. | He's **not standing**. | sit → sit**ting** |
| It's **starting**. | It's **not ending**. | wave → wav**ing** |
| We're **holding** scarves. | We're **not waving**. | |
| They're **playing** soccer. | They're **not playing** tennis. | |

**A** Complete Claudio's text messages with the present continuous forms of the verbs. Then compare with a partner.

1.
Where are you, Tim?
I **'m looking** _____
(look) for you. The game
_____
(start), but my favorite
player _____
(not / play) right now. Please
text me.

2.
Amy and
I _____
(watch) the game. But
where are you, Tim?
We _____
(sit) in row 56. Wait!
I _____
(get) a message. Is it you?

3.
Amy and I _____
(hold) signs.
We _____
(wave) in front of the TV
cameras. Can you see us?

**B Pair work** Make ten sentences about people in your class with the present continuous. Tell your partner.

*"I'm sitting behind Eva. Lily and Mei are wearing sweaters."*

# 4 Listening Someone is . . .

🔊 Listen to the sound effects. What is happening? Circle the correct answers.

1. Someone is (watching a game) / watching a movie.
2. Someone is **getting up** / **going to bed**.
3. Someone is **walking** / **running**.
4. Some people are **playing tennis** / **playing soccer**.
5. The game is **starting** / **ending**.

# 5 Speaking Guess the action.

**Group work** Perform an action. Your group guesses it. Take turns.

| | | |
|---|---|---|
| cook | run | stand |
| play tennis | sit | watch TV |
| play the guitar | sleep | wave |

A: *You're dancing.*
B: *No, I'm not.*
A: *You're playing soccer.*
B: *Yes, that's right.*

# 6 Keep talking!

Go to page 144 for more practice.

I can *describe what people are doing right now.* ✓

# B | *I can't talk right now.*

## 1 Interactions  Can you talk?

**A** Look at the pictures. What is Amanda doing?

**B** 🔊 Listen and practice.

**Amanda:** Hello?
**Justin:** Hi, Amanda. It's Justin. Is this a
good time to talk?

**Amanda:** Oh, sorry. I can't talk right now.
I'm cooking dinner. Can I call
you back?
**Justin:** OK, sure. Talk to you later.
**Amanda:** Thanks. Bye.

**C** 🔊 Listen to the expressions. Then practice the conversation again with the
new expressions.

| Asking if someone can talk now |
| --- |
| Is this a good time to talk?<br>Can you talk right now?<br>Do you have a minute? |

| Explaining that you can't talk now |
| --- |
| I can't talk right now.<br>I'm busy right now.<br>This isn't a good time. |

**D** **Pair work** Practice the conversation again with the reasons below.

clean                do my homework        play volleyball        wait for the doctor

## 2 **Listening** Do you have a minute?

**A** 🔊 Listen to four phone conversations. Number the questions you hear from 1 to 4.

_____ Can you talk right now?    _____ Is this a good time to talk?

_____ Is this a good time?    _1_ Do you have a minute?

**B** 🔊 Listen again. Why can't each person talk right now? Write the reason.

1. Eric _is having dinner_____ .    3. Ji-won _____ .
2. Renee _____ .    4. Carmen _____ .

## 3 **Speaking** Role play

**A** Complete the sentences with reasons why you can't talk on the phone.

I'm watching _____ .    I'm eating _____ .

I'm playing _____ .    I'm _____ .

**B Pair work** Role-play the situations. Then change roles.

**Student A:** Answer the phone. Explain that you can't talk now and say why. Use the reasons from Part A.

**Student B:** Call Student A. Identify yourself and ask if he or she can talk right now.

I can ask if someone can talk now.  ☑

I can explain why I can't talk on the telephone.  ☑

# C These days

## 1 Vocabulary Activities

**A** 🔊 Listen and repeat.

create a website

learn to drive

look for a job

study for an exam

study Italian

take a dance class

take tennis lessons

tutor a student

**B Pair work** Which activities are fun? Which are not fun? Compare answers with a partner.

## 2 Conversation Old friends

🔊 Listen and practice.

**Jill:** Long time no see, Wendy!
**Wendy:** Oh, hi, Jill.
**Jill:** What are you doing these days?
**Wendy:** I'm learning to drive. I'm also tutoring a student. Oh, and I'm taking a dance class.
**Jill:** You sound really busy.
**Wendy:** I am. How about you, Jill? Are *you* doing anything special these days?
**Jill:** Yes, I am. I'm studying Italian.
**Wendy:** Really? Why are you studying Italian?
**Jill:** Because . . . Oh, my phone is ringing. Hello? Sorry, Wendy. It's my new friend, Luigi.
**Wendy:** Oh.
**Jill:** *Ciao, Luigi! Come stai?*

# 3 Grammar 🔊 **Present continuous questions**

What **are** you **doing** these days?
 I'**m learning** to drive.
What class **is** Wendy **taking**?
 She'**s taking** a dance class.
Where **are** they **studying**?
 They'**re studying** online.

**Are** you **doing** anything special these days?
 Yes, I **am**.  No, I'**m not**.
**Is** she **tutoring** a student?
 Yes, she **is**.  No, she'**s not**.
**Are** they **taking** tennis lessons?
 Yes, they **are**.  No, they'**re not**.

**A** Complete the questions with the present continuous forms of the verbs.
Then compare with a partner.

1.  __Are__ you _taking_ (take) music lessons these days?
2. What classes _____ you _____ (take)?
3. _____ you and your friends _____ (buy)
   CDs these days?
4. What _____ your classmates _____ (learn)
   in this class?
5. What languages _____ you _____ (study)?
6. _____ you _____ (learn) to drive?

**B Pair work** Ask and answer the questions in Part A. Answer
with your own information.

# 4 Pronunciation Intonation in questions

🔊 Listen and repeat. Notice the intonation of *yes / no* and *Wh-* questions.

Are you watching a lot of TV?   What TV shows are you watching?

# 5 Speaking Busy lives

**Class activity** Add two activities to the chart. Then find classmates who are doing
each thing these days. Write their names, and ask questions for more information.

| Are you . . . these days? | Name | Extra information |
|---|---|---|
| studying another language | | |
| reading a good book | | |
| watching a lot of TV | | |
| taking any fun classes | | |
| downloading a lot of music | | |
| | | |
| | | |

# 6 Keep talking!

Go to page 145 for more practice.

I can describe what people are doing these days. ☑

## 1 Reading ◄))

**A** What are you and your classmates doing right now?

**B** Read the status updates. Which two people are waiting for other people?

### Status Updates

SIGN UP   SIGN IN   SEARCH

#### What are you doing?

**Donna Bristol** I'm standing under the JB Cola sign on Main Street. I'm waiting for my friend Hank. But Hank is never late! Hank?
Apr 19 8:33 p.m.

**Hank Jones** I'm standing in line. Donna, please wait!! I'm in a store on First Avenue. The line isn't moving.
Apr 19 8:50 p.m.

**Fernando Sanchez** I'm studying English. I'm doing grammar exercises on my DVD-ROM. I'm getting them all correct. Yay!
Apr 19 9:05 p.m.

**Zack Parker** I'm enjoying Singapore!! I love vacations! How are my friends in Chicago doing?
Apr 19 9:17 p.m.

**Hee-jin Park** I'm having a great evening. I'm at my favorite restaurant with my two friends Alex and Eddie. We're waiting for dessert.
Apr 19 9:28 p.m.

**Jessica King** I'm looking for a good French dictionary. I'm taking a French class and need help with my vocabulary.
Apr 19 9:44 p.m.

**Arthur Henderson** I'm waiting for my daughter to come home. It's almost 10:00 p.m. Where are you, Lisa? You know the rules!
Apr 19 9:58 p.m.

**Lisa Henderson** I'm at a basketball game. Sorry, Dad. My favorite player is playing. 15 more minutes??
Apr 19 10:02 p.m.

**C** Read the updates again. Complete the sentences with first names.

1. ___Zack___ is on vacation.
2. _____ is having dinner.
3. _____ is standing in line.
4. _____ is watching a basketball game.
5. _____ and _____ are students.
6. _____ is studying English.

**D Pair work** How often do you write messages like the ones above? What do you write about? Tell your partner.

*"I love status updates. I write them twice a day. I usually write about the new music I find online."*

## 2 **Writing** My status update

**A** Write a status update about what you're doing right now or these days.

> *josie9:* *I'm studying Italian on the weekends.*

**B Group work** Pass your paper to the classmate on your right. Read and respond to your classmate's update. Continue to pass, read, and respond to each update three times.

> *josie9:* *I'm studying Italian on the weekends.*
>
> *93arren:* *I'm not studying Italian, but I'm learning to drive.*

## 3 **Speaking** Makoto's Desk

**Group work** Look at Makoto's desk. What do you think he's doing these days?

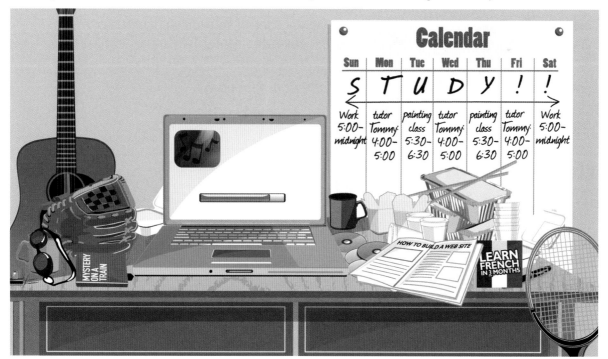

**A:** *I think he's studying French.*
**B:** *Right. And he's taking a painting class.*
**C:** *Do you think he's drinking a lot of coffee?*

> I can *discuss what people are doing.* ☑

# Wrap-up

## 1 Quick pair review

**Lesson A**  **Do you remember?** Complete the sentences with the correct prepositions. You have one minute.

1. The ball is _____ the bench.

2. The ball is _____ the bench.

3. The ball is _____ the bench.

4. The ball is _____ the bench.

**Lesson B**  **Brainstorm!** Make a list of phone expressions. How many do you know? You have two minutes.

**Lesson C**  **Find out!** What are two things both you and your partner are doing these days? You have one minute.

A: *What are you doing these days?*
B: *I'm taking tango lessons. Are you?*
A: *No, I'm not.*

**Lesson D**  **Guess!** Describe the clothes and actions of someone in your class, but don't say his or her name! Can your partner guess the name? Take turns. You have two minutes.

A: *He's wearing a baseball cap and talking to Angela right now.*
B: *Is it Sebastian?*
A: *Yes, it is.*

## 2 In the real world

Go to a mall or park. What are people doing? Write about them.

> *People in the Park*
> *I am in the park. Two women are walking. One woman is wearing a red T-shirt. A man is sitting next to me. He is eating his lunch. He is also . . .*

# Past experiences

## Warm-up

Dennis
Age 16

SMITH ACCOUNTING

Dennis Smith
*President*

Luz
Age 14

English

luz

**A** Look at the pictures. Make three sentences about each one.

**B** How are *you* different now?

**Last weekend**

# 1 Vocabulary Weekend activities

**A** 🔊 Listen and repeat.

listen to music

play basketball

play in a band

shop for new clothes

stay home

stay out late

visit relatives

watch an old movie

**B Pair work** Do you do any of the activities in Part A? When do you do them? Tell your partner.

*"My friends and I usually play basketball on Saturday mornings."*

# 2 Language in context Carmen's weekend

**A** 🔊 Listen to Carmen talk about last weekend. Number the pictures from 1 to 3.

1. Last Saturday morning, my brother Pedro called me. We talked for hours. I uploaded some photos, and I listened to music.

2. I stayed out late on Saturday night. Pedro and I watched an old movie. We laughed a lot. We loved it!

3. On Sunday afternoon, I stayed home. I watched another movie. I didn't like the ending at all. I cried.

1

**B** What about you? What do you usually do on weekends?

## 3 Grammar 🔊 | Simple past regular verbs

| | | Spelling |
|---|---|---|
| I **listened** to music last Saturday. | I **didn't watch** a movie. | stay → stay**ed** |
| You **stayed** home. | You **didn't stay** out late. | love → love**d** |
| He **called** me on Saturday. | He **didn't call** me on Sunday. | cry → cr**ied** |
| We **laughed**. | We **didn't cry**. | shop → shop**ped** |
| They **stayed** out late. | They **didn't stay** at home. | |

**A** Write sentences about the things Pedro did and didn't do last weekend.

*Things to Do*

✓ call Carmen    ✗ listen to music

✓ watch a movie    ✓ upload photos

✗ play basketball    ✗ shop for new clothes

1. *Pedro called Carmen.*
2. _____
3. _____
4. _____
5. _____
6. _____

**B Pair work** Make true sentences about your weekend with the past forms of the verbs in Part A. Tell your partner.

## 4 Pronunciation Simple past -ed endings

**A** 🔊 Listen and repeat. Notice that some verbs have an extra syllable in the simple past tense.

| Same syllable (most verbs) | Extra syllable (verbs ending in *t* and *d*) |
|---|---|
| call / called | chat / chat·ted |
| listen / listened | start / start·ed |
| play / played | upload / upload·ed |

**B** 🔊 Listen. Complete the chart with the correct verbs.

download / downloaded    shop / shopped    visit / visited
post / posted    stay / stayed    watch / watched

## 5 Speaking A fun weekend

**A** Complete the phrases with your own ideas.

chat with _____    exercise _____    study _____    visit _____
cook _____    look for _____    talk to _____    walk to _____

**B Pair work** Tell your partner about the things you did and didn't do last weekend. Use the phrases from Part A to help you.

A: *I chatted online with my friends last weekend. How about you?*
B: *I didn't chat online with my friends, but I called them.*

## 6 Keep talking!

Go to page 146 for more practice.

*I can say what I did last weekend.* ☑

## 1 Interactions   Expressing surprise

**A** Look at the pictures. What do you think Ted and Valerie are talking about?

**B** 🔊 Listen and practice.

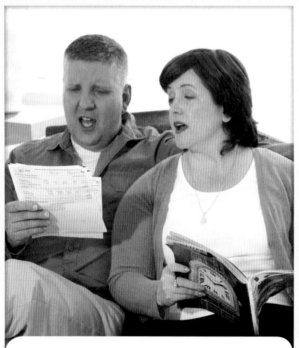

**Ted:** I checked our phone bill this morning.
**Valerie:** Uh-huh.
**Ted:** It's usually $59 a month, but this month it's $590.

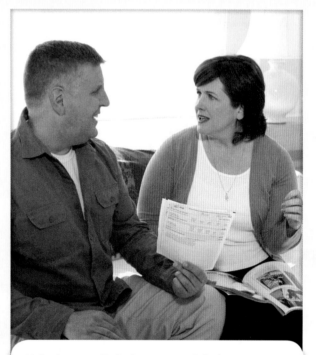

**Valerie:** Really? That's not right!
**Ted:** I know. I didn't pay it. I called the phone company, and they fixed it.
**Valerie:** Oh, that's good.

**C** 🔊 Listen to the expressions. Then practice the conversation again with the new expressions.

### Showing that you're listening

Uh-huh.
Oh?
Oh, yeah?

### Expressing surprise

Really?
What?
You're kidding!

**D** Check (✓) the best responses. Then practice with a partner.

| | | |
|---|---|---|
| 1. I watched a movie last night. | ✓ Uh-huh. | ☐ Really? |
| 2. I downloaded 500 songs yesterday. | ☐ You're kidding! | ☐ Oh? |
| 3. I didn't study for the big test. | ☐ Oh, yeah? | ☐ What? |
| 4. I played tennis with my friends on Sunday. | ☐ You're kidding! | ☐ Oh, yeah? |

## 2 Listening What a week!

**A** 🔊 Listen to Diana tell her friend about the past week. Number the pictures from 1 to 4.

1

**B** 🔊 Listen again. What surprises Diana's friend? Complete the sentences.

1. Diana didn't _____**answer**_____ three _____**questions**_____ .
2. Diana's _____ boyfriend _____ her.
3. Julie didn't _____ the _____ .
4. Diana _____ home on _____ .

## 3 Speaking Really?

**A** Match the sentences. Then compare with a partner.

1. Last night, I studied for my English test for five hours. __b__
2. I just checked my email. _____
3. Last week, I downloaded two movies. _____
4. On Thursday, I started a new class. _____

a. I watched them with my dad.
b. But I didn't get a good score.
c. I'm learning Chinese.
d. I have 100 new messages.

**B Pair work** Role-play the situations in Part A. Then change roles.

**Student A:** Say the lines from Part A.
**Student B:** Show interest or express surprise.

> **A:** *Last night, I studied for my English test for five hours, but I didn't get a good score.*
> **B:** *You're kidding! Why not?*

**C Pair work** Role-play new situations. Use your own ideas.

*I can show that I'm listening.* ☑
*I can express surprise.* ☑

# *Did you make dinner last night?*

## 1 Vocabulary Things to do

**A** 🔊 Listen and repeat.

do laundry

do the dishes

get a haircut

go grocery shopping

have a party

make dinner

see a play

see friends

sleep

**B Pair work** How often do you do the things in Part A? Tell your partner.

*"I do laundry once a week. I do the dishes every day. . . ."*

## 2 Conversation Last night

🔊 Listen and practice.

**Mindy:** Hi, Pete. Did you see Jennifer last night?
**Pete:** Yes, I did. But the day didn't go so well.
**Mindy:** Really? What happened?
**Pete:** Well, I did my laundry yesterday morning, but my favorite white shirt turned pink.
**Mindy:** You're kidding!
**Pete:** Then I got a haircut, but I really didn't like it.
**Mindy:** Oh, yeah? Did you make dinner for Jennifer?
**Pete:** Well, I slept for a while, so I didn't go grocery shopping.
**Mindy:** Oh. Did you eat anything?
**Pete:** Yeah, we did. Jennifer bought a pizza for us.
**Mindy:** Really?

## 3 Grammar ◄)) **Simple past irregular verbs; yes / no questions**

I **saw** Jennifer last night.
She **bought** a pizza.
They **ate** a pizza.

I **didn't see** Jennifer last week.
She **didn't buy** soup.
They **didn't eat** salad.

**Did** you **see** Jennifer last night?
　Yes, I **did**.　　No, I **didn't**.
**Did** she **buy** dinner?
　Yes, she **did**.　No, she **didn't**.
**Did** they **eat** dinner?
　Yes, they **did**.　No, they **didn't**.

**A** Complete the conversation with the simple past tense forms of the verbs. Then practice with a partner.

A: Hey, Pablo. _Did_ you _do_ (do) today's homework?
B: No, I _didn't_ . I _____ (not / have) time.
A: Really? Why not?
B: I _____ (see) some friends yesterday. We _____ (eat) lunch, and then we _____ (go) to the mall.
A: Oh, yeah? _____ you _____ (buy) any clothes?
B: I _____ (not / buy) anything! So, _____ you _____ (do) *your* homework?
A: Yes, I did. And no, you can't see it!

◄)) **Common irregular verbs**

buy → **bought**　　have → **had**
do → **did**　　make → **made**
drink → **drank**　　meet → **met**
drive → **drove**　　read → **read**
eat → **ate**　　see → **saw**
fall → **fell**　　sleep → **slept**
get → **got**　　take → **took**
go → **went**　　write → **wrote**

Go to page 152 for a list of more irregular verbs.

**B** Put the words in order to make questions.
Then compare with a partner.

1. last night / you / see / did / your friends　　_Did you see your friends last night?_
2. go / last weekend / you / did / grocery shopping　_____
3. watch / you / a movie / did / last night　_____
4. yesterday / stay home / you / did　_____
5. make dinner / did / on Thursday / you　_____
6. you / did / last Saturday / have a party　_____

**C Pair work** Ask and answer the questions in Part B. Answer with your own information.

A: *Did you see your friends last night?*
B: *Yes, I did. I saw two friends. We ate out at a restaurant.*

## 4 Speaking Did you?

**A Pair work** Add two past time expressions to the list. Then ask and answer *Did you . . . ?* questions with each time expression. Take notes.

A: *Did you make dinner last night?*
B: *Yes, I did. Did you do laundry last night?*
A: *No, I didn't.*

| Past time expressions | |
|---|---|
| last night | last week |
| yesterday | last weekend |

**B Group work** Tell your group about your partner's answers. Did anyone do anything interesting?

## 5 Keep talking!
Go to page 147 for more practice.

*I can talk about routine events in the past.*

# D I saw a great movie.

## 1 Reading )))

**A** Do you ever read blogs? What kinds of blogs do you read?

**B** Read Matt's blog. Who liked the movie?

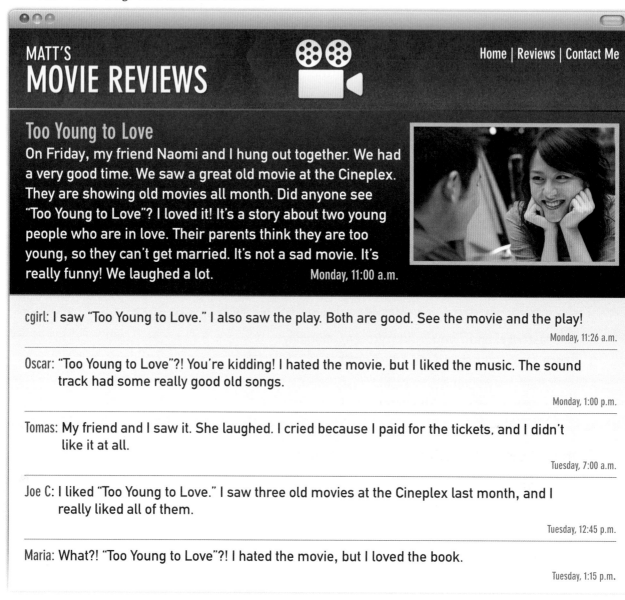

MATT'S
**MOVIE REVIEWS**                                                    Home | Reviews | Contact Me

**Too Young to Love**
On Friday, my friend Naomi and I hung out together. We had
a very good time. We saw a great old movie at the Cineplex.
They are showing old movies all month. Did anyone see
"Too Young to Love"? I loved it! It's a story about two young
people who are in love. Their parents think they are too
young, so they can't get married. It's not a sad movie. It's
really funny! We laughed a lot.                   Monday, 11:00 a.m.

cgirl: I saw "Too Young to Love." I also saw the play. Both are good. See the movie and the play!
                                                                                Monday, 11:26 a.m.

Oscar: "Too Young to Love"?! You're kidding! I hated the movie, but I liked the music. The sound
        track had some really good old songs.
                                                                                 Monday, 1:00 p.m.

Tomas: My friend and I saw it. She laughed. I cried because I paid for the tickets, and I didn't
        like it at all.
                                                                                Tuesday, 7:00 a.m.

Joe C: I liked "Too Young to Love." I saw three old movies at the Cineplex last month, and I
        really liked all of them.
                                                                               Tuesday, 12:45 p.m.

Maria: What?! "Too Young to Love"?! I hated the movie, but I loved the book.
                                                                                Tuesday, 1:15 p.m.

**C** Read the blog again. Correct the false sentences.

1. Matt saw the movie on ~~Saturday~~. _Matt saw the movie on Friday._
2. Oscar hated the music. _____
3. Tomas liked *Too Young to Love*. _____
4. Joe C didn't see any movies at the Cineplex last month. _____
5. Maria hated the book *Too Young to Love*. _____

**D Pair work** Do you or your friends ever post your everyday activities on a blog?
What do you post? Tell your partner.

*"My friend Rosa has a blog. She posts news about her neighborhood once a week."*

## 2 **Writing** A blog post

**A** Choose one day last week. Complete the chart with information about the things you did that day.

| Day | Activities | Places | Other information |
|-----|-----------|--------|-------------------|
|     |           |        |                   |
|     |           |        |                   |

**B** Write a blog post about that day. Use the model and your answers in Part A to help you.

**C** **Pair work** Share your post. Ask and answer questions for more information.

*"Did you have a good time? Did you eat out?"*

*Friday*
*After class, I met my friend Terry. We went shopping at the mall. I bought a new watch. I didn't pay much for it, but I really like it. I went home at 8:00 p.m.*

## 3 **Listening** A busy week

**A** 🔊 Listen to Matt talk about last week. What activities did he do? Check (✓) the correct answers.

- ☐ did laundry
- ☑ got up early
- ☐ got up late
- ☐ made dinner
- ☐ played soccer
- ☐ played the guitar
- ☐ read books
- ☐ stayed out late
- ☐ worked

**B** 🔊 Listen again. What activities did Matt enjoy? Circle the activities above.

## 4 **Speaking** I played in a band last year.

**A** **Class activity** Add two past activities to the chart. Then find classmates who did each thing. Write their names, and ask questions for more information.

| Find someone who . . . | Name | Extra information |
|------------------------|------|-------------------|
| bought a cell phone last year |  |  |
| got a haircut last week |  |  |
| saw a friend yesterday |  |  |
| made dinner last night |  |  |
| watched a game on TV last weekend |  |  |
| wrote a blog post yesterday |  |  |
|  |  |  |
|  |  |  |

**A:** *Did you buy a cell phone last year, Alex?*
**B:** *Yes, I did.*

**B** Share your information.

*"Alex bought a cell phone last year."*

*I can talk about past activities.* ☑

# Wrap-up

## 1 Quick pair review

**Lesson A** **Find out!** What are three things both you and your partner did after class yesterday? What are three things you didn't do? You have two minutes.

**A:** *I walked home after class yesterday. Did you?*
**B:** *Yes, I did. I watched TV at home. Did you?*
**A:** *No, I didn't. I listened to music.*

**Lesson B** **Do you remember?** Circle the correct answers. You have two minutes.

1. **A:** I listened to all of Taylor Swift's songs today.
   **B:** Oh? / You're kidding! All of them? She has a lot!

2. **A:** Janet uploaded photos from the party.
   **B:** Uh-huh. / Really? I know. I looked at them this morning.

3. **A:** Charlie's band played at The Red Room downtown on Saturday night!
   **B:** What? / Oh? No way! That's so cool! I didn't know that.

4. **A:** I visited my grandmother last weekend.
   **B:** You're kidding! / Oh, yeah? How is she doing?

**Lesson C** **Test your partner!** Say eight irregular verbs in the simple present. Can your partner write the simple past forms of the verbs correctly? Check his or her answers. You have two minutes.

1. _____   3. _____   5. _____   7. _____
2. _____   4. _____   6. _____   8. _____

**Lesson D** **Guess!** Make two true sentences and one false sentence about your activities last week. Can your partner guess the false sentence? Take turns. You have two minutes.

**A:** *I watched 20 movies last week. I played basketball in the park. I saw a play.*
**B:** *You didn't watch 20 movies.*
**A:** *You're right. I only watched 12.*

## 2 In the real world

Did anyone else do the same things as you yesterday? Go online and find three English-speaking bloggers who did the same activities as you yesterday. Then write about them.

- What activities did both you and the bloggers do yesterday?
- What are the bloggers' names?
- Where are they from?

> *Bloggers and Me*
> *I played basketball yesterday. Three bloggers also played basketball yesterday.*
> *Diego is from California. He played basketball with his brother.*

# Getting away

## Warm-up

**A** Do you know any of these places? Which ones?

**B** What are some popular places to visit in your country? in your city?

# A *Where were you?*

## 1 Vocabulary Adjectives

**A** 🔊 Listen and repeat.

exciting / fun / great      all right / OK / so-so      awful / terrible

boring      interesting      noisy      quiet

**B Pair work** Think of things that each adjective describes. Discuss your ideas.

**A:** *Sports are exciting.*
**B:** *Basketball is exciting, but I think soccer is boring.*

## 2 Language in context Quick getaways

**A** 🔊 Listen to four people talk about recent trips. Number the pictures from 1 to 4.

1. We went on a school trip last week. We went to a theater and saw an exciting play. The actors were great.

                              – *Olivia*

2. We just had a three-day weekend. I went away with my family. It was a fun trip, but our hotel wasn't very nice. In fact, it was terrible.

                              – *Ichiro*

3. I was at my brother's apartment last weekend. He doesn't have a TV or a computer. It was quiet and kind of boring.

                              – *Brian*

4. My friend and I went on a day trip last week. We took a local bus to an old town. The bus was awful and noisy, but the trip was interesting. Look what I bought!

                              – *Eleanor*

1

**B** Did each person like his or her trip? Why or why not?

# 3 Grammar 🔊 Past of *be*

| Where **were** you last weekend? | **Was** your trip interesting? | |
| --- | --- | --- |
| I **was** at my brother's apartment. | Yes, it **was**. | No, it **wasn't**. |
| **How was** your weekend? | **Were** the people nice? | |
| It **was** quiet and kind of boring. | Yes, they **were**. | No, they **weren't**. |

| *I / he / she / it* | *you / we / they* | *Contractions* | |
| --- | --- | --- | --- |
| **was** | **were** | wasn't = was not | weren't = were not |

**A** Complete the guest comment card with *was, were, wasn't,* or *weren't*. Then compare with a partner.

> 🙞 **Guest comments** 🙜
>
> My wife, son, and I _____*were*_____ guests at your hotel last week. Unfortunately,
> we _____ happy with our room. The room _____ clean, and the
> beds _____ awful. And the room _____ near the street. The noise
> _____ terrible in the early morning. But the people at the hotel _____
> great, so that _____ good!

**B** Read the answers. Write the questions. Then practice with a partner.

1. *How was your weekend?*_____    It was great.
2. _____    Yes, my weekend was interesting.
3. _____    I was on a trip.
4. _____    No, I wasn't at the theater on Friday.
5. _____    Yes, I was at home on Sunday afternoon.
6. _____    My parents were in Tahiti.

**C Pair work** Ask and answer the questions in Part B. Answer with your own information.

# 4 Speaking Where were you last Friday night?

**A Pair work** Interview your partner. Take notes.

| Where were you . . . ? | Location | Extra information |
| --- | --- | --- |
| at this time yesterday | | |
| on your birthday | | |
| on New Year's Eve | | |
| last Friday night | | |

**B Group work** Tell your group about your partner's answers. Who was in an interesting place? Who did interesting things?

# 5 Keep talking!

Go to page 148 for more practice.

I can *describe where I was in the past.* ✓

# B That's great!

## 1 Good news, bad news

**A** 🔊 Listen and repeat.

I got a promotion.  I lost my wallet.  I missed my flight.  I was sick.  I won a contest.

**B Pair work** Which things are good news? Which are bad news? Can you think of other examples? Discuss your ideas.

## 2 Interactions   Reacting to news

**A** 🔊 Listen and practice.

**Meg:** Did you have a good weekend?
**Joe:** Yes! I won a trip in a contest, so I went away last weekend.
**Meg:** Really? That's great!

**Joe:** And how was your weekend?
**Meg:** It wasn't so good. I lost my wallet.
**Joe:** Oh, no! What happened?

**B** 🔊 Listen to the expressions. Then practice the conversation again with the new expressions.

### Reacting to good news

That's great!
That's excellent!
That's awesome!

### Reacting to bad news

Oh, no!
That's too bad.
That's terrible!

**C Pair work** Practice the conversation again with the examples from Exercise 1. React to the news.

**A:** *Did you have a good weekend?*
**B:** *Yes! I got a promotion, so I went shopping.*

# 3 Listening  A short trip

**A** 🔊 Listen to Sam tell a friend about a short trip. Number the pictures from 1 to 6.

**B** 🔊 Listen again. Was Sam's trip great, good, bad, or awful?

# 4 Speaking  That's . . . !

**A** Write three good things and three bad things that happened to you last week.

| | Good things that happened | Bad things that happened |
|---|---|---|
| 1. | | |
| 2. | | |
| 3. | | |

**B Class activity** Ask your classmates about their week. React to the news.

> **A:** *Did you do anything interesting last week?*
> **B:** *Well, I started a new job.*
> **A:** *That's excellent!*
> **B:** *Yeah. But I lost my cell phone.*
> **A:** *That's terrible!*

*I can react to news.* ✓

# C My vacation

## 1 Vocabulary Vacation activities

**A** 🔊 Listen and repeat.

buy souvenirs

go sightseeing

go to a festival

go to the beach

relax

shop in markets

take a tour

take pictures

**B Pair work** Did you do any of the activities in Part A on your last vacation? Tell your partner.

*"On my last vacation, I bought souvenirs and took pictures. I didn't go to the beach."*

## 2 Conversation Back from vacation

🔊 Listen and practice.

**Dave:** How was your vacation, Kate?
**Kate:** Oh, it was exciting. We had a great time.
**Dave:** Where did you go?
**Kate:** I went to Veracruz, Mexico.
**Dave:** That's great. Who did you travel with?
**Kate:** My sister.
**Dave:** When did you get back?
**Kate:** Last night. I got home at midnight.
**Dave:** Really? That's late! So, what did you do there?
**Kate:** Well, we went to a festival called *Carnaval*. We also shopped in local markets and took lots of pictures. Look, I bought you a souvenir.
**Dave:** Thanks! I love it!

## 3 Grammar  🔊    Simple past *Wh*- questions

| | |
|---|---|
| **Where did** you **go** on vacation? <br>    I went to Veracruz, Mexico. <br> **When did** you **get** back? <br>    Last night. <br> **Who did** you **travel** with? <br>    My sister. | **What did** you **do** there? <br>    We went to a festival and shopped. <br> **Why did** you **go** to Veracruz? <br>    Because the festival is famous. <br> **How did** you **get** to Veracruz? <br>    By plane. |

Match the questions and the answers. Then practice with a partner.

1. Where did you go on vacation? __*f*__
2. Who did you go with? _____
3. When did you get back? _____
4. What did you do on vacation? _____
5. Why did you go to Vietnam? _____
6. How did you travel in Vietnam? _____

a. We got back last week.
b. We took the bus and the train.
c. We relaxed and took pictures.
d. Because I have friends there.
e. I went with my brother.
f. I went to Vietnam.

## 4 Pronunciation   Reduction of *did you*

**A** 🔊 Listen and repeat. Notice how *did you* is pronounced /dɪdʒə/ after *Wh*- question words.

Where **did you** go?     What **did you** do?     When **did you** get back?

**B Pair work** Practice the questions in the grammar chart. Reduce *did you* to /dɪdʒə/ after *Wh*- question words.

## 5 Speaking   What a vacation!

**A** Answer the questions.

- Where did you go on your last vacation? _____
- Who did you go with? _____
- When did you go? _____
- What did you do there? _____
- How did you travel? _____
- Did you buy anything? _____
- What did you like about the vacation? _____
- What didn't you like about the vacation? _____

**B Group work** Tell your group about your last vacation. Ask and answer questions for more information.

## 6 Keep talking!

Go to page 149 for more practice.

fly → flew

take a boat → took a boat

*I can* talk about my last vacation. ✓

111

# D Travel experiences

## 1 Reading 🔊

**A** How often do you go on vacation? Where do you go?

**B** Read the travel blog posts. What country is each person visiting?

**travel tales**

I'm here in Chiang Mai, Thailand. Yesterday, I went on a short elephant ride. There was a man on the elephant in front of me. His name was Alan Johnson. My name is Alan Johnson, too! _____

Alan Johnson    Posted on October 12, 10:30 a.m.

My sister and I are in Paris, France. It's our first trip overseas. We went to an outdoor café the other day, and Johnny Depp was at the next table. How exciting! _____

Mary O'Connor    Posted on October 14, 6:48 p.m.

I'm here with my parents at a hotel in Miami, Florida. We came to visit our relatives. We all went to bed last night at about midnight. At 3:00 in the morning, we heard a fire alarm. _____

Anita Gonzalez    Posted on October 15, 8:06 a.m.

I'm in Granada, Nicaragua. I came here to help build houses. It's a great country. We finished our first house yesterday. We're not staying in a hotel. We're staying in a school. ___1___

Diane Nicholson    Posted on October 21, 9:12 p.m.

**C** Read the blog posts again. What is the last sentence of each post? Number the posts from 1 to 4.

1. Last night, we all slept in one big room!

2. He was nice to us, and I have a cool photo now.

3. I can't believe that we have the same name!

4. We ran down to the street and were fine.

**D Pair work** What adjectives describe each travel experience? Discuss your ideas.

A: *I think Alan Johnson's trip was very exciting!*
B: *Me, too. I love elephants, and Thailand is an interesting country.*

## 2 Listening Three different trips

**A** 🔊 Listen to three people talk about their vacations. How do they describe them? Check (✓) the correct answers.

| | How were their vacations? | | What was one thing they liked? |
|---|---|---|---|
| 1. | ☐ awful | ✓ great | *shopping* |
| | ☐ boring | ☐ so-so | |
| 2. | ☐ fun | ☐ OK | |
| | ☐ interesting | ☐ terrible | |
| 3. | ☐ awful | ☐ exciting | |
| | ☐ boring | ☐ great | |

**B** 🔊 Listen again. What did they like about their trips? Write one thing for each person in the chart.

## 3 Writing and speaking A postcard

**A** Read Sofia's postcard to Jack about her vacation.

> Dear Jack,
>
> Linda and I are having a great time here in Morocco. We took a train from Casablanca to Marrakech yesterday. Last night, we went to a big "souk," or market. We walked around the market for hours! I bought a nice souvenir for you!
>
> See you soon!
> Sofia

**B** Write a postcard to a friend or family member about an experience you had on vacation. Use the model in Part A to help you.

**C Class activity** Post your postcards around the room. Read your classmates' postcards. Then write questions about five postcards that interest you.

> 1. Eddie – What did you buy for your sister?
>
> 2. Jung-woo – Who did you travel with?
>
> 3. Marcus – When did you take this vacation?

**D Class activity** Find the classmates who wrote the five postcards. Ask them your questions.

> **A:** Eddie, what did you buy your sister?
> **B:** I bought a scarf.
> **A:** I see, thanks. Excuse me, Jung-woo, who did you travel with?

*I can describe a vacation.* ☑

# Wrap-up

## 1 Quick pair review

**Lesson A Brainstorm!** Make a list of adjectives. How many do you know? You have one minute.

**Lesson B Do you remember?** Check (✓) the correct answers. You have one minute.

1. I won a free ticket to Jamaica.  ☑ That's great!  ☐ Oh, no!
2. I lost my cell phone.  ☐ That's terrible!  ☐ That's excellent!
3. My sister missed her flight.  ☐ That's awesome.  ☐ That's too bad.
4. Charlie met Leonardo DiCaprio.  ☐ Oh, no!  ☐ That's great!

**Lesson C Find out!** What are two things both you and your partner did on your last vacation? You have two minutes.

A: *Did you go sightseeing on your last vacation?*
B: *Yes, I did. How about you?*
A: *Yes, I went sightseeing, too.*

**Lesson D Test your partner!** Describe a vacation. Can your partner draw a postcard of your vacation? Check his or her drawing. You have two minutes.

*"Last year, my sister and I went to Madrid, Spain. We shopped in El Rastro Market and went to art museums."*

## 2 In the real world

Do you ever read travel blogs? Go online and find a travel blog in English. Then write about it.

- Where did the blogger go?
- When did he or she go there?
- What did he or she do there?

> *Kelly's Travel Blog*
> *Kelly is a blogger from Canada. Last week, she went on vacation to Scotland. She went sightseeing in Glasgow. She went to . . .*

# Time to celebrate

| LESSON **A** | LESSON **B** | LESSON **C** | LESSON **D** |
|---|---|---|---|
| • Months and dates<br>• *Be going to*;<br> *yes / no* questions | • Declining an<br> invitation<br>• Accepting an<br> invitation | • Party checklist<br>• *Wh-* questions<br> with *be going to*;<br> object pronouns | • Reading: "Birthday<br> Traditions"<br>• Writing: A thank-<br> you note |

## Warm-up

<u>graduation</u>

_____

_____          _____

**A** Label the pictures with the correct words.

> birthday   ✓graduation   holiday   wedding

**B** What special events do you celebrate?

# A I'm going to get married.

## 1 Vocabulary Months and dates

**A** 🔊 Listen and repeat.

| January | February | March | April | May | June |
|---------|----------|-------|-------|-----|------|
| July | August | September | October | November | December |

| | | | | | | | |
|---|---|---|---|---|---|---|---|
| **1st** first | **9th** ninth | **17th** seventeenth | **25th** twenty-fifth |
| **2nd** second | **10th** tenth | **18th** eighteenth | **26th** twenty-sixth |
| **3rd** third | **11th** eleventh | **19th** nineteenth | **27th** twenty-seventh |
| **4th** fourth | **12th** twelfth | **20th** twentieth | **28th** twenty-eighth |
| **5th** fifth | **13th** thirteenth | **21st** twenty-first | **29th** twenty-ninth |
| **6th** sixth | **14th** fourteenth | **22nd** twenty-second | **30th** thirtieth |
| **7th** seventh | **15th** fifteenth | **23rd** twenty-third | **31st** thirty-first |
| **8th** eighth | **16th** sixteenth | **24th** twenty-fourth | |

**B Class activity** When is your birthday? Stand in the order of your birthdays, from the first to the last in the year.

A: *My birthday is July twenty-eighth.*
B: *Mine is July twentieth. You're next to me.*

## 2 Language in context Special days

**A** 🔊 Listen to three people talk about special days. What are the dates of the special days?

I'm going to graduate from high school on June 8th. I'm going to start college in September.

– Sarah

My eightieth birthday is on August 21st. I'm going to go skydiving for the first time. I can't wait!

– Walter

My boyfriend, Kenta, and I are going to get married on October 16th. We're going to have a big wedding.

– Mari

**B** What about you? What days of the year are special to you? Why?

116

# 3 Grammar 🔊 | *Be going to; yes / no* questions

| | |
|---|---|
| I**'m going to graduate** on June 8th. | **Are** you **going to start** college? |
| I**'m not going to start** college in July. | Yes, I am.   No, I'm not. |
| Walter**'s going to go** skydiving. | **Is** Walter **going to go** skydiving? |
| He**'s not going to play** basketball. | Yes, he is.   No, he isn't. |
| Mari and Kenta **are going to get** married. | **Are** they **going to have** a big wedding? |
| They**'re not going to have** a small wedding. | Yes, they are.   No, they aren't. |

**A** Complete the conversation with the correct forms of *be going to.*
Then practice with a partner.

A: __*Are*__ you *going to graduate* (graduate) from college
this year?

B: Yeah, on May 30th. My parents _____
(have) a big party for me.

A: Great! _____ the party _____ (be) at
their house?

B: No, it _____ (not / be) at the house.
They _____ (have) it at a restaurant.

A: _____ you _____ (get) a job right away?

B: No, I'm not. First, I _____ (travel).
Then I _____ (look) for a job.

**B Pair work** Ask and answer three *Are you going to . . . ?* questions.
Answer with your own information.

# 4 Pronunciation Reduction of *going to* before verbs

**A** 🔊 Listen and repeat. Notice how *going to* is reduced to /ɡənə/ in informal
spoken English.

Are you **going to** do anything special?   Yes. I'm **going to** go skydiving.

**B Pair work** Practice the sentences in the grammar chart. Reduce *going to*
to /ɡənə/.

# 5 Speaking Three special days

**A** Write the dates and your plans for three special days or holidays next year.

| | Special day: _____ | Special day: _____ | Special day: _____ |
|---|---|---|---|
| Dates | | | |
| Plans | | | |

**B Pair work** Tell your partner about your special days. Ask and answer questions
for more information.

# 6 Keep talking!

Go to page 150 for more practice.

| *I can* talk about my plans for specific dates. | ✓ |

117

# B  *Sure. I'd love to.*

## 1 Interactions | Invitations

**A** How often do you go to the movies with your friends?

**B** 🔊 Listen and practice.

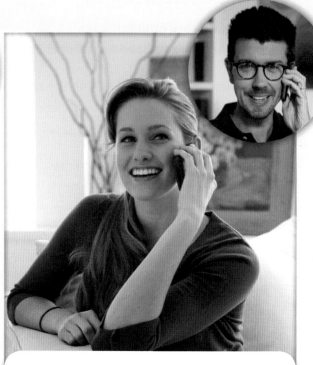

**Bill:** Hello?
**Brandon:** Hey, Bill. It's Brandon. Listen, do you want to see a movie tonight?
**Bill:** Tonight? I'm sorry. I can't.
**Brandon:** Oh, OK. Well, maybe some other time.

**Melissa:** Hello?
**Brandon:** Hi, Melissa. This is Brandon. Do you want to see a movie tonight?
**Melissa:** A movie? Sure. I'd love to.
**Brandon:** Great.

**C** 🔊 Listen to the expressions. Then practice the conversation again with the new expressions.

| Declining an invitation |
| --- |
| I'm sorry. I can't.
I'm afraid I can't.
I'm really sorry, but I can't. |

| Accepting an invitation |
| --- |
| Sure. I'd love to.
Sounds good.
Yeah. That sounds great. |

**D Pair work** Practice the conversations again with the activities below.

| get some ice cream | hang out | play video games | watch a DVD |

**A:** *Hello?*
**B:** *Hey, Bill. It's Brandon. Listen, do you want to get some ice cream tonight?*

## 2 Listening I'd love to, but . . .

**A** 🔊 Listen to four people invite their friends to do things tonight. Number the pictures from 1 to 4.

**B** 🔊 Listen again. Do the friends accept or decline the invitations? Check (✓) the correct answers.

1. ✔ accept    2. ☐ accept    3. ☐ accept    4. ☐ accept
    ☐ decline       ☐ decline       ☐ decline       ☐ decline

## 3 Speaking Do you want to hang out?

**Class activity** "Call" your classmates and invite them to do something with you right now. Your classmates accept the invitations or decline them with excuses. Use the ideas below or your own ideas.

| Possible things to do | Possible excuses | Responses to excuses |
|---|---|---|
| go out for coffee | I'm cooking dinner. | Oh, that's OK. |
| go to a party | I'm not feeling well. | Maybe next time. |
| see a movie | I'm eating lunch. | I'm sorry you can't make it. |
| go to the mall | I'm studying for an exam. | OK, I understand. |
| hang out | I'm doing my homework. | That's all right. |
| go shopping | I'm working late tonight. | No problem. |

A: *Hello?*
B: *Hi, it's me. Do you want to go to the mall?*
A: *I'm really sorry, but I can't. I'm not feeling well.*
B: *OK, I understand. Maybe next time.*

*I can accept or decline an invitation.* ☑

# C Planning a party

## 1 Vocabulary Party checklist

**A** 🔊 Match the things on the checklist and the pictures. Then listen and check your answers.

**THINGS TO DO**

1. [g] bake a cake
2. [ ] buy a gift
3. [ ] choose the music
4. [ ] decorate the room
5. [ ] make a guest list
6. [ ] plan the menu
7. [ ] prepare the food
8. [ ] send invitations

a — John Hee-jin Miguel

b — Invitation

c — Menu Sandwiches Ice Cream Soda

d

e — HAPPY BIRTHDAY

f

g

h

**B** **Pair work** When is a good time to do each thing in Part A? Discuss your ideas.

| 2 weeks before the party | 2–3 days before the party | the morning of the party |
| 1 week before the party | the day before the party | 1 hour before the party |

"A good time to make a guest list is two weeks before the party."

## 2 Conversation I can bake!

🔊 Listen and practice.

**Andrea:** We have a lot of things to do for Eric's birthday party. Look, I made a checklist.
**Mark:** Good idea. Who's going to help us?
**Andrea:** Rosario. She's going to send the invitations.
**Mark:** How is she going to send them?
**Andrea:** By email.
**Mark:** Good. That's easy. What are we going to buy for Eric?
**Andrea:** Let's get him a sweater.
**Mark:** Great. Who's going to bake the cake?
**Andrea:** I'm going to bake it.
**Mark:** Um, do you think that's a good idea?
**Andrea:** Hey, I can bake!
**Mark:** OK.

# 3 Grammar 🔊 Wh- questions with be going to; object pronouns

| **What** are we going to buy **Eric**? | Let's get **him** a sweater. |
|---|---|
| **Who**'s going to bake **the cake**? | Andrea's going to bake **it**. |
| **How** is she going to send **the invitations**? | She's going to send **them** by email. |

| Subject | I | you | he | she | it | we | they |
|---|---|---|---|---|---|---|---|
| Object | me | you | him | her | it | us | them |

**A** Complete the conversation with the correct forms of *be going to*. Then practice with a partner.

A: What time __are__ you __going to go__ (go) to Eric's birthday party?
B: I _____ (go) to the party at 6:45.
A: How _____ you _____ (get) there?
B: My friend Jason _____ (drive). Do you want a ride?
A: Um, sure, thanks! What _____ you _____ (do) after the party?
B: Jason and I _____ (go) out. I think we _____ (see) a movie.

**B** Rewrite the sentences. Use object pronouns. Then compare with a partner.

1. He's not going to invite Mary. _He's not going to invite her._____
2. Let's call Bill and Ami again. _____
3. I'm going to see Eric tomorrow. _____
4. He's going to help Debbie and me. _____
5. We're going to buy the present tomorrow. _____
6. Call Rosario at 5:00. _____

**C Class activity** Ask your classmates what they're going to do tonight. Answer with your own information.

# 4 Speaking Let's decide together.

**A Pair work** Discuss the situations.

| Your classmate Masao is in the hospital. He has nothing to do. What are you going to bring him? | You're planning your friend's birthday party. Where is it going to be? What are you going to eat and drink? | You want music for your teacher's birthday party. What songs are you going to play? How are you going to listen to them? |
|---|---|---|

A: *What are we going to bring to Masao?*
B: *Let's bring him a new video game.*
A: *That's a great idea. How about . . . ?*

**B Group work** Share your ideas with another pair. Ask and answer questions for more information.

# 5 Keep talking!

Go to page 151 for more practice.

I can *discuss and agree on plans.* ☑

# D Birthdays

## 1 Reading 🔊

**A** What was the last party you went to? What did you do at the party?

**B** Read the article. Which birthdays are special in each country?

# Birthday Traditions
*around the world*

### Nigeria
In Nigeria, the first, fifth, tenth, and fifteenth birthdays are very special. To celebrate these birthdays, people have big parties and invite up to 100 people. They eat "jollof rice." This is rice with tomatoes, red peppers, onions, and cassava, a kind of potato.

### Japan
The third, fifth, and seventh birthdays are very important in Japan. Every year on November 15th, children of these ages celebrate the *Shichi-go-san* (Seven-five-three) Festival. They usually wear traditional clothes and eat "thousand-year candy" for a long life.

### Ecuador
In Ecuador, a family has a big party when a girl turns 15 years old. The birthday girl wears a dress, and her father puts her first pair of high-heeled shoes on her. Then he dances with her. Fourteen other girls dance with fourteen other boys at the same time.

### South Korea
Parents in South Korea sometimes try to guess a child's future on his or her first birthday. They put the child in front of some objects, such as a book and a coin. They wait to see which object the child takes. For example, a book means the child is going to be a teacher. A coin means the child is going to have a lot of money.

**C** Read the article again. Answer the questions.

1. On special birthdays, what do Nigerian children eat? _They eat "jollof rice."_
2. Who celebrates *Shichi-go-san*? _____
3. Who dances with a 15-year-old Ecuadorian girl at her birthday party? _____
4. How do South Korean parents guess a child's future? _____

**D Pair work** How did you celebrate your last birthday? Tell your partner.

*"I celebrated my last birthday with my friends. We ate out at a nice restaurant."*

# 2 Listening Sweet 16

**A** 🔊 Listen to Amanda, a 16-year-old American girl, describe her "Sweet 16" birthday party. Check (✓) the true sentences.

1. ✓ Amanda's birthday is July 14th.

2. ☐ ~~Her parents~~ *She* made a guest list.

3. ☐ She sent the invitations.

4. ☐ She and her father decorated the room.

5. ☐ She had pizza, ice cream, and cake.

6. ☐ Forty of her friends came.

7. ☐ She got a gift from her parents.

8. ☐ She's going to have a party on her 18th birthday.

**B** 🔊 Listen again. Correct the false sentences.

# 3 Writing A thank-you note

**A** Think of a birthday gift (or any gift) you received. Answer the questions.

- What is the gift? _____
- Who is it from? _____
- Why did you get it? _____
- What do you like about it? _____

**B** Write a thank-you note for the gift. Use the model and your answers in Part A to help you.

**C** **Group work** Share your thank-you notes. Did any of you write about similar gifts?

*Dear Liz,*

*Thanks a lot for the birthday gift. I love the sweater. Blue and green are my favorite colors. Thank you for coming to my party!*

*Thanks again,*
*Sun-hee*

# 4 Speaking How we celebrate

**A** **Group work** Discuss the ways people celebrate birthdays in your culture. Use the questions below and your own ideas.

- Which birthdays are very special?
- Do people celebrate with family, friends, or both?
- What do people eat and drink?
- What do people do?
- Do they give gifts? What kinds of gifts?
- How do you usually celebrate birthdays?

**B** **Group work** Tell your group how you are going to celebrate your next birthday. Are you going to do any of the things you discussed in Part A?

a birthday party in Mexico

I can *describe birthday traditions in my culture.* ☑

123

# Wrap-up

## 1 Quick pair review

**Lesson A** **Guess!** Say three dates when you are going to do something special. Can your partner guess what you are going to do? Take turns. You have three minutes.

**A:** *I'm going to do something special on June 17th.*
**B:** *Are you going to graduate?*
**A:** *Yes, I am!*

**Lesson B** **Do you remember?** Read the sentences. Write A (accepting an invitation), D (declining an invitation), or E (making an excuse). You have one minute.

1. I'd love to. _____
2. I'm studying for an exam. _____
3. That sounds great. _____
4. I'm really sorry, but I can't. _____
5. I'm working late tonight. _____
6. I'm afraid I can't. _____

**Lesson C** **Brainstorm!** Make a list of things you do to plan a party. How many do you know? You have two minutes.

**Lesson D** **Find out!** What are three activities both you and your partner do on your birthdays? You have two minutes.

**A:** *I eat cake on my birthday. Do you?*
**B:** *Yes, I eat cake, too.*

## 2 In the real world

When is your birthday? Go online and find information in English about two important events that happened that day. Then write about them.

- Where did the events happen?
- Who participated in the events?
- Why were the events important?

*My Birthday*
*My birthday is December 17th. On this day in*
*1903, the Wright brothers flew an airplane for*
*12 seconds. This was important because . . .*

# Name circle

**A Group work** Stand in a circle. Go around the circle and say your first names.
Repeat your classmates' names before you say your own name.

My name is Eduardo.

His name is Eduardo.
My name is Ming-mei.

His name is Eduardo.
Her name is Ming-mei.
My name is Adam.

His name is Eduardo.
Her name is Ming-mei.
His name is Adam.
My name . . .

**B Group work** Go around the circle again. Repeat your classmates' full names.

A: *My name is Eduardo Sanchez.*
B: *His name is Eduardo Sanchez. My name is Ming-mei Lee.*
C: *His name is Eduardo Sanchez. Her name is Ming-mei Lee. My name . . .*

# Entertainment awards

### Student A

**Pair work** You and your partner have pictures of the same people, but some of the jobs and cities are different. Ask questions to find the differences. Circle them.

**A:** *Is Antonio Loren a model in your picture?*
**B:** *Yes, he is.*
**A:** *OK. That's the same. Is he from Rome?*
**B:** *No, he's from Milan. That's different.*

# Around the world

**A** Create a "new" identity. Write your new name and the country and city you are from.

Name: _____

Country: _____

City: _____

Vancouver, Canada
Chicago, U.S.
Toronto, Canada
London, England
Berlin, Germany
Moscow, Russia
Paris, France
New York, U.S.
Madrid, Spain
Rome, Italy
Beijing, China
Los Angeles, U.S.
Seoul, South Korea
Tokyo, Japan
Miami, U.S.
Havana, Cuba
Cairo, Egypt
Delhi, India
Mexico City, Mexico
Santiago, Dominican Republic
Dakar, Senegal
Panama City, Panama
Bogotá, Colombia
Bangkok, Thailand
Nairobi, Kenya
Lima, Peru
São Paulo, Brazil
Sydney, Australia
Buenos Aires, Argentina
Cape Town, South Africa
Auckland, New Zealand

**B** **Group work** Interview four classmates. Complete the cards with their "new" identities.

Name: _____

Country: _____

City: _____

Name: _____

Country: _____

City: _____

Name: _____

Country: _____

City: _____

Name: _____

Country: _____

City: _____

**A:** *Hi. What's your name?*

**B:** *Hi. My name is Sophie Manet.*

**A:** *Where are you from, Sophie?*

**B:** *I'm from France.*

**A:** *Oh, you're French. What city are you from?*

**B:** *I'm from Paris.*

# Entertainment awards

## Student B

**Pair work** You and your partner have pictures of the same people, but some of the jobs and cities are different. Ask questions to find the differences. Circle them.

**A:** *Is Antonio Loren a model in your picture?*
**B:** *Yes, he is.*
**A:** *OK. That's the same. Is he from Rome?*
**B:** *No, he's from Milan. That's different.*

# Family tree

**A** Draw your family tree. Include your family members, their names, and their ages.

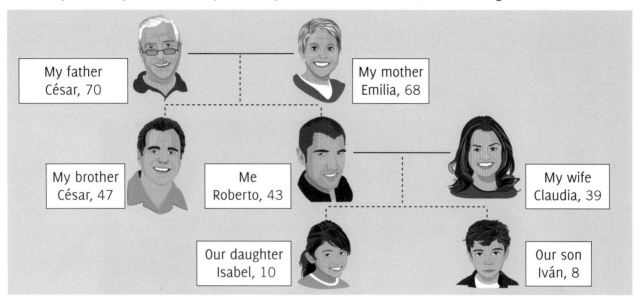

My father
César, 70

My mother
Emilia, 68

My brother
César, 47

Me
Roberto, 43

My wife
Claudia, 39

Our daughter
Isabel, 10

Our son
Iván, 8

**My Family Tree**

**B** **Pair work** Tell your partner about your family tree, but don't show it! Your partner draws it on another sheet of paper. Take turns.

A: *My grandfather is George. He's 72 years old. My grandmother is Anna.*
B: *How do you spell "Anna"?*
A: *A-N-N-A.*
B: *OK, thanks.*
A: *She's 68. Their kids are . . .*

**C** **Pair work** Compare your drawing with your partner's family tree. Are they the same?

# Cleaning the closet

**Pair work** Look at Dean and Lucy's closet. What things are in their closet?

**A:** *What's that?*
**B:** *It's a dictionary. What's that?*
**A:** *It's a cell phone. Hey, what are these?*

# What color?

## Student A

**A** **Pair work** You and your partner have pictures of the same people, but some of their clothes are different colors. Describe the clothing to find the differences. Circle them.

Alice
Ben
Cindy
Drew
Ellen
Fred
Frank

A: *In my picture, Alice's coat is blue and white.*
B: *That's the same in mine. And her pants are gray.*
A: *In my picture, her pants are green. That's different.*

**B** **Pair work** Cover the picture. What is the same? Answer with the information you remember.

A: *Alice's coat is blue and white.*
B: *Yes. And Ben's pants are . . .*

# What color?

### Student B

**A Pair work** You and your partner have pictures of the same people, but some of their clothes are different colors. Describe the clothing to find the differences. Circle them.

A: *In my picture, Alice's coat is blue and white.*
B: *That's the same in mine. And her pants are gray.*
A: *In my picture, her pants are green. That's different.*

**B Pair work** Cover the picture. What is the same? Answer with the information you remember.

A: *Alice's coat is blue and white.*
B: *Yes. And Ben's pants are . . .*

# Car, train, bus, or bicycle?

**A** Look at the ways people get to work in Los Angeles.

**How people in Los Angeles get to work**

| | |
|---|---|
| 65% | drive alone |
| 15% | drive with others |
| 10% | take the bus |
| 4% | walk |
| 1% | ride a bicycle |
| 5% | other |

*Source:* www.fhwa.dot.gov/ctpp/jtw/jtw4.htm

Note: % = percent

**B Pair work** Guess the ways people get to work in New York City. Complete the chart with the numbers. Then check your answers on the bottom of page 134.

| 1% | 6% | 6% | 8% | 8% | 14% | 25% | 32% |
|---|---|---|---|---|---|---|---|

**How people in New York City get to work**

| | |
|---|---|
| _____ % | drive alone |
| _____ % | drive with others |
| _____ % | take the bus |
| _____ % | walk |
| _____ % | take the subway |
| _____ % | take the train |
| _____ % | take a taxi |
| _____ % | other |

*Source:* www.fhwa.dot.gov/ctpp/jtw/jtw4.htm

**C Group work** Guess the ways people get to work where *you* live. Rank them from 1 to 8.

_____ drive alone  _____ ride a bicycle  _____ take the bus  _____ walk
_____ drive with others  _____ take a taxi  _____ take the train or subway  _____ other

A: *I think number 1 is "take the train or subway."*
B: *I agree. I think number 2 is "drive alone."*

# Routines

**A Class activity** Find classmates who do each thing. Write their names.

| Find someone who . . . | Name | Find someone who . . . | Name |
|---|---|---|---|
| gets up before 6:00 | | sleeps a lot on weekends | |
| studies in the morning | | walks to class | |
| takes a shower at night | | has a red cell phone | |
| has coffee at home | | studies on the bus | |
| reads every day | | takes a bath in the morning | |
| goes to bed early | | drives a sports car | |
| watches TV after midnight | | doesn't have a dictionary | |

take a shower

take a bath

drive a sports car

**A:** *Do you get up before 6:00, Donna?*
**B:** *No, I don't. I get up at 6:30.*
**A:** *How about you, Michael? Do you get up before 6:00?*
**C:** *Yes, I do.*

**B** Share your information.

**A:** *Michael gets up before 6:00.*
**B:** *And Angela gets up before 6:00. David studies in the morning.*

Answers to Keep talking! Unit 4 Lesson A, Part B (page 133): 25% drive alone, 6% drive with others, 14% take the bus, 8% walk, 32% take the subway, 8% take the train, 1% take a taxi, 6% other

# On the computer

**A** Add two more questions about online activities to the chart.

| Do you ever . . . ? | Name: _____ |
|---|---|
| read people's blogs | |
| buy books online | |
| use online dictionaries | |
| search the Internet in English | |
| check the weather online | |
| get directions online | |
| check movie times online | |
| | |
| | |

check the weather

get directions

check movie times

**B** **Pair work** Interview your partner. Complete the chart with his or her answers. Use adverbs of frequency.

A: *Naoko, do you ever read people's blogs?*
B: *Oh, yes. I often do. Do you?*
A: *I hardly ever do.*
B: *Do you ever . . . ?*

**C** **Pair work** Tell another classmate about your partner's answers.

A: *Naoko often reads people's blogs.*
B: *Sasha never does.*

# Follow-up questions

**A** Add two follow-up questions about each topic to the charts.

| Sports and games | Questions | Name: _____ |
|---|---|---|
| | Do you ever play sports? | |
| | What do you play? | |
| | Who do you play with? | |
| | | |
| | | |

| Shopping | Questions | Name: _____ |
|---|---|---|
| | Do you ever go shopping? | |
| | Where do you shop? | |
| | What do you buy there? | |
| | | |
| | | |

| Getting around | Questions | Name: _____ |
|---|---|---|
| | Do you ever take the bus? | |
| | Why do you take the bus? | |
| | When do you take it? | |
| | | |
| | | |

**B Class activity** Find a classmate who does each activity. Then ask the follow-up questions. Take notes.

A: *Do you ever play sports, Samantha.*
B: *Yes, I sometimes do.*
A: *What do you play?*
B: *I play tennis.*

**C** Share your information. What answers are popular in your class?

# Job details

**A** Look at the picture for two minutes. Try to remember the people's names, jobs, and other information.

**B** **Pair work** Cover the picture. Ask the questions and answer with the information you remember.

- What does Pam do?
- Where does she work?
- Who does she work with?
- What does Paul do?
- How does Jane get to work?

- What does Tommy do?
- Where does Mei-li work?
- What does she do?
- What company does Mitch work for?
- What does Carla do?

> **A:** *What does Pam do?*
> **B:** *I think she's a waitress.*
> **A:** *Yes, I think so, too. Where does she work?*

**C** **Pair work** Ask and answer two more questions about the picture.

# Start to finish

**Group work** Play the game. Put a small object on *Start*. Toss a coin.

 Move 1 space.         Move 2 spaces.

Heads                          Tails

Read the question. Can you do what it says? Take turns.

Yes. → Move ahead.        No. ← Move back.

# What's in your shopping basket?

**A** Choose seven items to put into your shopping basket. Circle them.

**B** **Pair work** Find out what is in your partner's basket. Can you make the dishes below with the food in your baskets?

**Stew**
beef
carrots
noodles

**Fruit smoothie**
apples
bananas
milk

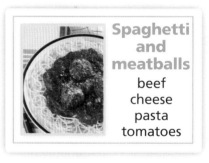

**Spaghetti and meatballs**
beef
cheese
pasta
tomatoes

A: *I have beef and noodles. Do you have any carrots?*
B: *Yes, I do. We can make stew!*

**C** **Pair work** What else can you make with the food in your baskets?

# How often do you eat standing up?

**Group work** Add two eating habits to the list. Then discuss how often you do each thing.

drink coffee in the morning

drink tea

eat alone

eat candy in class

eat fast food for breakfast

eat on the street

eat standing up

_____
(your own idea)

_____
(your own idea)

**A:** *Do you ever drink coffee in the morning?*
**B:** *Yes, I do.*
**C:** *How often do you drink coffee in the morning?*
**B:** *I drink coffee in the morning three times a week. How about you?*

# What's missing?

### Student A

**A Pair work** You and your partner have pictures of the same neighborhood, but different places are missing. Ask questions to get the names. Write them.

A: *What's across from the post office?*
B: *The gas station.*

**B Pair work** Cover the picture. Tell your partner six things you remember.

A: *The gas station is across from the post office.*
B: *That's right.*

# What's missing?

### Student B

**A Pair work** You and your partner have pictures of the same neighborhood, but different places are missing. Ask questions to get the names. Write them.

A: *What's next to the movie theater?*
B: *Parkview Hotel.*

**B Pair work** Cover the picture. Tell your partner six things you remember.

A: *Parkview Hotel is next to the movie theater.*
B: *That's right.*

## An unusual zoo

**Pair work** What's wrong at this zoo? Make ten sentences about the people, animals, and other things in the zoo. Use *There is . . .* , *There are . . .* , and prepositions of location.

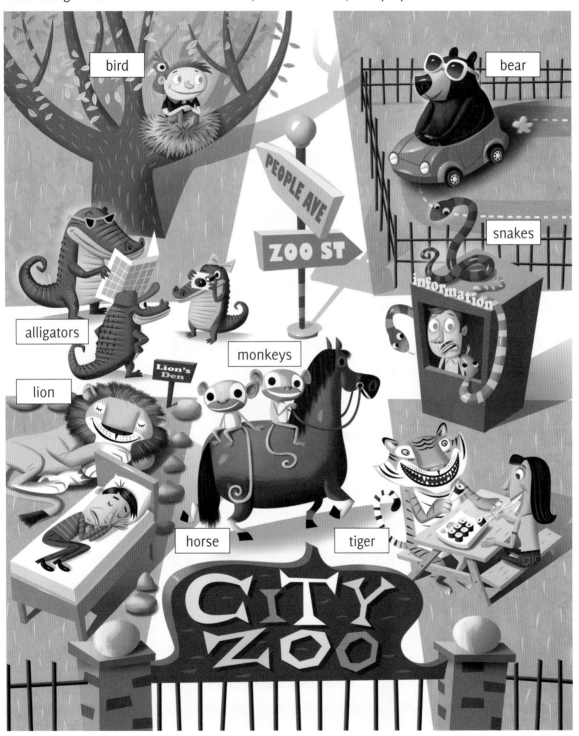

bird

bear

snakes

alligators

monkeys

lion

horse

tiger

*"There's a bear in the car."*

## Neighbors

**A Pair work** Look through the windows. What are the people doing?
Discuss your ideas.

A: *I think the man is doing his homework. What do you think?*
B: *I think he's writing a letter. He's sitting, too.*

**B Pair work** What are the people actually doing? Go to page 153 to check
your answers.

# Who is it?

**A** Write three sentences about what you're doing these days on three pieces of paper. Don't write your name!

| | | |
|---|---|---|
| *I'm tutoring a student.* | *I'm taking tennis lessons.* | *I'm not studying every night!* |

**B Group work** Put your papers on the table. Take one paper and read the sentences. Your group guesses the name. Take turns.

**A:** *This person is tutoring a student.*
**B:** *Is it Juliana?*
**C:** *No, it's not me!*
**D:** *Is it Kate?*

**C Group work** Discuss the activities you're doing these days. Ask and answer questions for more information.

**A:** *Who are you tutoring these days, Ken?*
**B:** *I'm tutoring a friend of mine. His name is Luke.*
**C:** *Are you tutoring him in English?*
**B:** *No, I'm not. I'm tutoring him in Japanese.*

## Picture story

**A Pair work** Look at the pictures of John and Alice Gordon. What did they do last weekend? Use the verbs to discuss your ideas.

| | | | | |
|---|---|---|---|---|
| clean | fix | play | stay out | watch |
| dance | paint | shop for | study | |

**A:** *John and Alice cleaned the house.*
**B:** *Alice fixed her bike.*

**B Pair work** Cover the pictures. What did John and Alice do last weekend? Answer with the information you remember.

# Memories

**Group work** Make five true sentences about your past activities with the phrases below. Your group asks three questions about each sentence for more information. Take turns.

| Yesterday | Last night | Last weekend | Last month | Last year |
|-----------|-----------|--------------|------------|-----------|
| I drank . . . | I ate . . . | I saw . . . | I bought . . . | I went . . . |
| I got up . . . | I went to bed . . . | I had . . . | I read . . . | I met . . . |
| I did . . . | I slept . . . | I drove . . . | I made . . . | I took . . . |

**A:** *Last night, I ate soup for dinner.*
**B:** *Did you eat in a restaurant?*
**A:** *No, I didn't. I ate at home.*
**C:** *Did you make the soup?*
**A:** *No, I didn't. My son made it.*
**D:** *Did you . . . ?*

# School trips

**A Pair work** Add three more questions about school or work trips to the list. Then interview your partner. Take notes.

1. What was your favorite school or work trip?

   _____

2. How old were you?

   _____

3. How was the trip?

   _____

4. Was there anything bad about the trip?

   _____

5. Did you take a bus there?

   _____

6. Were you there all day?

   _____

7. Did you buy anything?

   _____

8. _____

   _____

9. _____

   _____

10. _____

   _____

**B Pair work** Tell another classmate about your partner's answers.

*"Michi's favorite school trip was to a cookie factory. She was ten years old. The trip was . . ."*

# What a vacation!

**A** Look at the items from Maggie's vacation. Write five questions and answers about her vacation.

1. *Where did Maggie go on vacation?*
   *New York City.*
2. *What kind of music did she hear?*
   *Jazz music.*

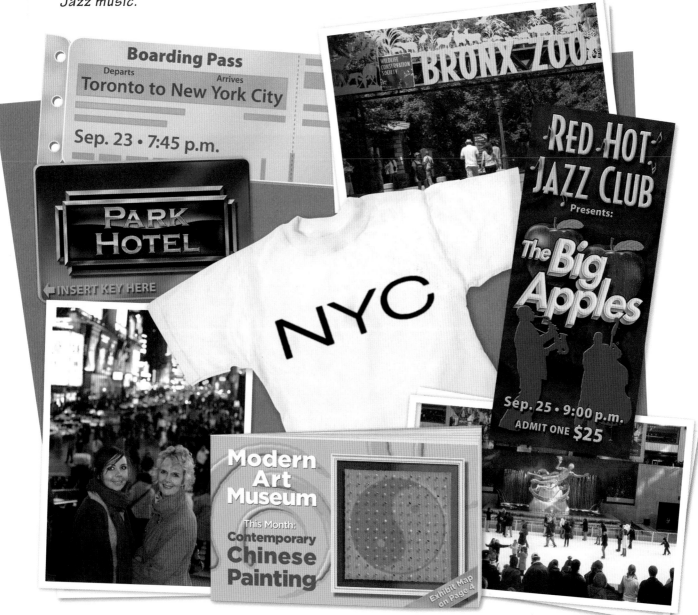

**B Group work** Cover the picture. Ask your questions. How many correct answers did your group get?

# This weekend

**A** Make eight true sentences about your plans with the phrases below.

| My plans | | |
|---|---|---|
| | dress up | |
| | eat out | |
| | go to a concert | tonight |
| | go to bed late | this evening |
| I'm going to | go to the mall | tomorrow |
| I'm not going to | go window-shopping | this weekend |
| | hang out | next Monday |
| | study | next Friday |
| | watch a movie | |
| | work | |

dress up

go to a concert

go window-shopping

**B** **Pair work** Tell your partner about your plans. Ask and answer questions for more information.

> A: *I'm going to go to bed late tonight.*
> B: *Are you going to watch a movie tonight?*
> A: *No, I'm not. I'm going to study.*

# Party planners

**A** **Group work** Plan an end-of-class party. Take notes.

| Date of party | Time of party | Place of party |
|---|---|---|
|  |  |  |

| Food and drink | Decorations | Music |
|---|---|---|
|  |  |  |

A: *When are we going to have our party?*
B: *Let's have it after class on Friday at 8:00.*
C: *OK. Now, where are we going to have it?*
D: *Let's have it here at the school.*

**B** **Class activity** Share your ideas. Ask and answer questions for more information.

A: *We're going to have our party on Friday at 8:00.*
B: *It's going to be here at our school.*
C: *Which room is the party going to be in?*

**C** **Class activity** Vote for your favorite plan.

# Irregular verbs

| Base form | Simple past |
|-----------|-------------|
| be | was, were |
| become | became |
| build | built |
| buy | bought |
| can | could |
| choose | chose |
| come | came |
| do | did |
| draw | drew |
| drink | drank |
| drive | drove |
| eat | ate |
| fall | fell |
| feel | felt |
| fly | flew |
| get | got |
| give | gave |
| go | went |
| hang | hung |
| have | had |
| hear | heard |
| hold | held |
| know | knew |
| leave | left |

| Base form | Simple past |
|-----------|-------------|
| lose | lost |
| make | made |
| meet | met |
| pay | paid |
| read | read |
| ride | rode |
| run | ran |
| say | said |
| see | saw |
| sell | sold |
| send | sent |
| sing | sang |
| sit | sat |
| sleep | slept |
| speak | spoke |
| spend | spent |
| stand | stood |
| swim | swam |
| take | took |
| teach | taught |
| think | thought |
| wear | wore |
| win | won |
| write | wrote |

# Answer key

**Keep talking!** Neighbors

# Credits

## Illustration credits

Peter Ellis: 7, 16, 26, 106, 144, 153; Tom Garrett: 25, 31, 35, 55, 65, 89, 130; John Goodwin: 4, 20, 93, 95, 129, 138 *(icons)*; Kim Johnson: 2, 3, 6, 10, 30, 40 *(bottom)*, 50, 59, 67, 70, 90, 99, 110, 131, 132, 146, 151; Dean MacAdam: 41, 47, 60, 69, 80, 85, 100, 120 *(bottom)*, 126, 127, 137, 143, 147; Michael Mantel: 39, 56, 109

Garry Parsons: 36, 46 *(bottom)*, 53, 86, 96, 116, 120 *(top)*, 125, 134, 145; Maria Rabinky: 15, 75, 76 *(top)*, 81, 141, 142; Cristina Sampaio: 40 *(top)*, 57, 87 *(bottom)*, 108, 140; Rob Schuster: 5, 27 *(bottom)*, 29, 46 *(top)*, 52, 78, 79, 119, 138 *(board)*, 149; Otto Steinenger: 27 *(top)*, 33

## Photography credits

8 ©Media Bakery; 9 ©Media Bakery; 10 *(clockwise from top left)* ©Everett Collection; ©Everett Collection; ©Petite Poupee/Flickr; ©Frederick M. Brown/Getty Images; ©Kris Connor/Getty Images; ©Jeff Christensen/AP Wide World Photo; 12 *(clockwise from top left)* ©Elisabetta Villa/Getty Images; ©Everett Collection; ©Scott Gries/Getty Images; ©Kevin Mazur/Getty Images; ©Jamie McDonald/Getty Images; ©GV Cruz/Getty Images; 13 *(top to bottom)* ©Allstar Picture Library/Alamy; ©Allstar Picture Library/Alamy; ©Jon Kopaloff/Getty Images; ©Jon Kopaloff/Getty Images; 17 ©Photo Library; 18 ©Alamy; 22 *(clockwise from top left)* ©Media Bakery; ©Photo Library; ©Alamy; ©Derek Trask/Alamy; 23 *(top row, left to right)* ©Jenny Acheson/Getty Images; ©Media Bakery; ©Golden Pixels/Alamy; ©Michael Newman/Photo Edit; *(bottom)* ©Media Bakery; 26 *(top row, left to right)* ©Istock; ©Istock; ©Shutterstock; ©Adventure House; *(middle row, left to right)* ©Shutterstock; ©Media Bakery; ©Istock; ©Istock; *(bottom row, left to right)* ©Istock; ©Shutterstock; ©Dorling Kindersley/Getty Images; 28 *(top row, left to right)* ©Shutterstock; ©Dorling Kindersley/Getty Images; ©Shutterstock; ©David Young-Wolff/Photo Edit; ©Shutterstock; *(bottom)* ©Frank Veronsky; 32 *(clockwise from top left)* ©Alamy; ©Lenscap/Alamy; ©Shutterstock; ©Shutterstock; ©Media Bakery; ©Urikiri-Shashin-Kan/Alamy; 33 *(clockwise from top left)* ©Dorling Kindersley/Getty Images; ©Istock; ©Istock; ©Shutterstock; ©Getty Images; ©Shutterstock; ©Shutterstock; ©Alamy; 34 *(clockwise from top left)* ©Shutterstock; ©Shutterstock; ©Helene Rogers/Alamy; ©Shutterstock; ©Shutterstock; ©Istock; 36 *(clockwise from top left)* ©Getty Images; ©Liu Xiaoyang/Alamy; ©Patrick Eden/Alamy; ©Tony Anderson/Getty Images; ©Alamy; ©Media Bakery; ©David Gee/Alamy; ©Alamy; 38 *(top two rows)* ©Shutterstock; *(bottom row)* ©Frank Veronsky; 39 ©Shutterstock; 42 *(top to bottom)* ©Shutterstock; ©Media Bakery; ©Istock; ©Media Bakery; ©Istock; ©Shutterstock; 44 *(all)* ©Shutterstock; 45 *(clockwise from top left)* ©Media Bakery; ©Media Bakery; ©Alex Segre/Alamy; ©Media Bakery; 46 *(middle row, left to right)* ©Camille Tokerud/Getty Images; ©Dreamstime; ©Media Bakery; 48 *(background store images)* ©Alamy; *(foreground people images)* ©Frank Veronsky; 49 *(all)* ©Shutterstock; 50 *(top row, left to right)* ©Photo Stock Israel/Alamy; ©Ryan McVay/Getty Images; ©Media Bakery; *(middle row, left to right)* ©Media Bakery; ©Alamy; ©Alamy; *(bottom row, left to right)* ©Robert Clayton/Alamy; ©David Sanger/Alamy; ©Perry Mastrovito/Getty Images; ©Alamy; ©Getty Images; 52 *(clockwise from top left)* ©Dreamstime; ©Norma Zuniga/Getty Images; ©David White/Alamy; ©Shutterstock; ©Alex Segre/Alamy; 53 *(left to right)* ©Kevin Foy/Alamy; ©Stephen Dunn/Getty Images; ©Alamy; ©Daniel Dempster/Alamy; 56 *(both)* ©Media Bakery; 58 *(top row)* ©Frank Veronsky; *(bottom row, left to right)* ©Golden Pixels/Alamy; ©Workbook Stock/Getty Images; ©Getty Images; ©Media Bakery; 60 *(clockwise from top left)* ©Media Bakery; ©Alamy; ©Alamy; ©Media Bakery; ©Media Bakery; ©Marmaduke St. John/Alamy; ©Media Bakery; ©Media Bakery; 62 *(top to bottom)* ©Media Bakery; ©Media Bakery; ©Getty Images; 63 *(left to right)* ©Media Bakery; ©China Photos/Getty Images; ©Media Bakery

66 *(bananas)* ©Veer; *(beans)* ©Bon Appetit/Alamy; *(pasta)* ©Inmagine; *(all other food)* ©Shutterstock; *(bottom row, left to right)* ©Chris Rout/Alamy; ©Getty Images; ©Alamy; 67 *(all)* ©Shutterstock; 68 ©Frank Veronsky; 70 *(sushi)* ©Veer; *(all other food)* ©Shutterstock; 72 *(clockwise from top left)* ©Veer; ©Shutterstock; ©Alamy; ©Judd Pilossof/Getty Images; 73 *(globe, food)* ©Shutterstock; *(man)* ©Adventure House; 77 *(left to right)* ©Media Bakery; ©Jeff Greenberg/Alamy; ©Cris Haigh/Alamy; ©Ian Dagnall/Alamy; 78 ©Frank Veronsky; 80 *(clockwise from top left)* ©Joe McBride/Getty Images; ©Alamy; ©Erik Dreyer/Getty Images; ©Tomas Abad/Alamy; ©Alex Segre/Alamy; ©Wolfgang Kaehler/Alamy; ©Alamy; ©Frans Lemmens/Alamy; 82 *(all)* ©Stephen Saks/Alamy; 83 *(left to right)* ©Rob Walls/Alamy; ©Javier Larera/Photo Library; ©Ian Shaw/Photo Library; 88 *(clockwise from top left)* ©Alamy; ©Media Bakery; ©Getty Images; ©Alamy; ©Bruce Laurance/Getty Images; ©Alamy; 90 *(clockwise from top left)* ©Alamy; ©Alamy; ©Leander Baerenz/Getty Images; ©Alamy; ©Media Bakery; ©Alamy; ©Hans Neleman/Getty Images; ©Andrea Matone/Alamy; 91 ©Alamy; 92 *(top to bottom)* ©Media Bakery; ©Shutterstock; ©Alamy; ©Kaz Chiba/Getty Images; ©Media Bakery; ©Paul Williams/Alamy; ©Ron Chapple/Getty Images; ©Shutterstock; 96 *(clockwise from top left)* ©Alamy; ©Media Bakery; ©Neil Beckerman/Getty Images; ©Charles Gullung/Getty Images; ©Inmagine; ©Getty Images; ©Alamy; ©Alamy; 98 ©Frank Veronsky; 100 *(top row, left to right)* ©Media Bakery; ©Media Bakery; ©Jim West/Alamy; *(middle row, left to right)* ©Getty Images; ©Getty Images; ©Alexey Stiop/Alamy; *(bottom row, left to right)* ©Vehbi Koca/Alamy; ©Media Bakery; ©Media Bakery; 102 ©Media Bakery; 105 *(Costa Rica beach)* ©Franck Guiziou/Getty Images; *(Golden Gate Bridge)* ©Getty Images; *(trolley)* ©Mitchell Funk/Getty Images; *(all others)* ©Shutterstock; 106 *(left to right)* ©Gavin Hellier/Alamy; ©Alamy; ©Lebrecht Music and Arts Photo Library/Alamy; ©Red Cover/Alamy; 108 ©Frank Veronsky; 110 *(clockwise from top left)* ©Otto Stadler/Getty Images; ©Andrew Watson/Getty Images; ©Alamy; ©Bill Bachmann/Alamy; ©Alamy; ©Yadid Levy/Alamy; ©JL Images/Alamy; 111 *(both)* ©Shutterstock; 112 *(top to bottom)* ©Corbis; ©Jeffrey Mayer/Getty Images; ©Media Bakery; ©Jeff Greenberg/Alamy; 113 ©Rohan/Getty Images; 115 *(clockwise from top left)* ©Media Bakery; ©Peter Titmuss/Alamy; ©Media Bakery; ©Hiroko Masuike/Getty Images; 117 ©Media Bakery; 118 ©Frank Veronsky; 122 *(clockwise from top left)* ©Flickr; ©Jon Arnold Images Ltd./Alamy; ©Amanda Ahn/Alamy; ©Adam Eastland/Alamy; 123 ©ML Pearson/Alamy; 133 *(top to bottom)* ©Media Bakery; ©David Grossman/Alamy; 139 *(fish)* ©Holdger Burmeister/Alamy; *(noodles)* ©Dreamstime; *(rice)* ©David Lee/Alamy; *(cheese)* ©Media Bakery; *(beans)* ©Alistair Heap/Alamy; *(milk, spaghetti, cereal)* ©Shutterstock; *(all other food, top group)* ©Shutterstock; *(bottom row, left to right)* ©Valerie Janssen/Getty Images; ©Media Blitz Images Limited/Alamy; ©Alamy; 148 *(left to right)* ©Alibi Productions/Alamy; ©Media Bakery; 149 *(clockwise from top left)* ©Alamy; ©Sandra Baker/Alamy; ©Edward Simons/Alamy; 150 *(left to right)* ©Media Bakery; ©Alamy; ©Neil Beckerman/Getty Images